Better Homes and Gardens®

Cooking for Two

Credits

On the cover
Simple-to-Fix Supper Menu features:
Pork Chops with Mushroom Gravy
Zucchini-Carrot Sauté
Mashed Potatoes with Fines Herbes
Strawberry Meringue Puffs
(see recipes, pages 14 and 15)

BETTER HOMES AND GARDENS® BOOKS
Editor: Gerald M. Knox
Art Director: Ernest Shelton
Managing Editor: David A. Kirchner

Food and Nutrition Editor: Doris Eby
Department Head Cook Books: Sharyl Heiken
Senior Food Editor: Elizabeth Woolever
Senior Associate Food Editors: Sandra Granseth, Rosemary C. Hutchinson
Associate Food Editors: Jill Burmeister, Julia Martinusen, Linda Miller, Alethea Sparks, Marcia Stanley, Diane Yanney
Recipe Development Editor: Marion Viall
Test Kitchen Director: Sharon Stilwell
Test Kitchen Home Economists: Jean Brekke, Kay Cargill, Marilyn Cornelius, Maryellyn Krantz, Marge Steenson

Associate Art Director (Managing): Randall Yontz
Associate Art Directors (Creative): Linda Ford, Neoma Alt West
Copy and Production Editors: Nancy Nowiszewski, Lamont Olson, Mary Helen Schiltz, David A. Walsh
Assistant Art Directors: Faith Berven, Harijs Priekulis
Graphic Designers: Mike Burns, Alisann Dixon, Mike Eagleton, Lynda Haupert, Deb Miner, Lyne Neymeyer, Trish Church-Podlasek, Bill Shaw, D. Greg Thompson

Editor in Chief: Neil Kuehnl
Group Editorial Services Director: Duane L. Gregg
Executive Art Director: William J. Yates

General Manager: Fred Stines
Director of Publishing: Robert B. Nelson
Director of Retail Marketing: Jamie Martin
Director of Direct Marketing: Arthur Heydendael

Cooking for Two
Editor: Julia Martinusen
Copy and Production Editor: Nancy Nowiszewski
Graphic Designer: Lynda Haupert

Our seal assures you that every recipe in *Cooking for Two* is endorsed by the Better Homes and Gardens Test Kitchen. Each recipe is tested for family appeal, practicality, and deliciousness.

Contents

We've taken the guesswork out of cooking for two people. No more will you have to divide recipes meant for six servings or eat the same casserole three nights in a row. Every recipe in this book is geared to serve just the two of you.

The book is divided into two chapters: a menu chapter and a recipe chapter. The menu chapter reflects current cooking trends—everything you could want from gourmet to low-cost cooking. To aid you in your food preparation, the recipe chapter contains several colorful how-to photographs and helpful food preparation tips.

As we developed these recipes, we tried to eliminate one of the biggest problems with cooking in small quantities—leftover ingredients. However, there are occasions when leftovers are unavoidable. To help you use the remaining amount of an ingredient, we've indexed other recipes calling for that ingredient in the back of the book.

MENUS

The following menus cater to almost any meal situation you might encounter. Our Deluxe Dinners will help you celebrate an occasion with someone special. The Deluxe Menu pictured at

left features Chicken Marsala, Fettuccine with Olives, and Creamy Orange Zabaglione (see all of the recipes on page 11). But if you're looking for something less involved, try one of our Simple-to-Fix Suppers.

When you don't have a minute to spare, whip up one of our Beat-the-Clock Menus. To give you an idea of the amount of time you'll need, we've listed preparation timings for each recipe and menu. Or, if you know you'll be busy right up to the last moment, reserve some time beforehand to prepare one of our Make-Ahead Menus. We've given you the advance and final preparation timings to help you fit the meal preparation into your schedule.

Just in case you're skimming some of the fat off your food budget, we've included three delicious Low-Cost Meals that you can prepare quite reasonably. And for those days when you want a light yet satisfying meal, we've created some Calorie-Trimmed Meals. We've tallied the calorie counts for each recipe and the total meal. We think you'll be pleasantly surprised.

Deluxe Dinners

MENU

Spring Aspic

**Fillets of Sole
with Shrimp Sauce**

Boiled Sliced Potatoes

Steamed Asparagus

**French Bread with
Herb Butter**

Raspberry Chantilly

White or Rosé Wine

Celebrate a special occasion by serving one of these elegant dinners that we've designed just for you. To make the evening even more special, you can plan your atmosphere ahead of time. Create a mood with table settings, wine, lighting, and music.

Experiment with various tablecloths and place mats. Try matching some prints and plain fabrics to add interest to your overall color scheme. Fold napkins into intriguing shapes or use napkin rings.

For decoration, you can make two small individual arrangements of dried or fresh flowers instead of one large centerpiece.

When choosing wine, consider your tastes as well as the character of your meal. Generally, dry white wines complement the delicate flavors of veal, poultry, and seafood, while dry red wines will match the stronger flavors of beef and spicier fare. Rosé wines go well with almost any dinner.

And be sure to serve hot foods in warm dishes and chilled foods or wine in cold dishes or glasses.

Timetable

• **Several hours** before serving, thaw frozen fish and berries (if making Raspberry Chantilly).
• Chill the wine.
• Prepare the vegetables for the Spring Aspic.
• Prepare the aspic and chill.
• Prepare Raspberry Chantilly or Peach Chantilly and chill.
• **Thirty minutes** before serving, prepare the Herb Butter in a 350° oven. Turn the oven to 425° to cook the fish.
• Steam asparagus spears. Slice and boil potatoes.
• Bake the fish while preparing the sauce.
• Pour the sauce over the fish and finish baking.
• Spread the Herb Butter on the French bread. Serve any leftover butter on the boiled potato slices, if desired.

French Bread with Herb Butter

Pipe or spoon any leftover Herb Butter onto boiled potato slices—

- ¼ **cup butter *or* margarine**
- ¼ **teaspoon dried thyme, crushed**
- ¼ **teaspoon ground sage**
- 1 **small loaf French bread**

To soften the butter or margarine, cut into pieces. Place in a heat-proof bowl in a cool oven. Turn the oven to 350°; heat for 3 minutes.

Transfer the butter or margarine to a cool bowl to prevent melting. Stir thyme and sage into the softened butter or margarine. Slice the bread in half lengthwise. Spread the herb butter on both halves of the bread; replace top half. Makes 2 servings.

Fillets of Sole with Shrimp Sauce

8 ounces fresh *or* frozen
 sole fillets (2 fillets)
½ cup fresh, frozen, *or*
 canned tiny shelled
 shrimp*
1½ teaspoons lemon juice
 Salt
 Pepper
2 tablespoons snipped
 parsley
½ teaspoon dry mustard
1 teaspoon cornstarch
½ cup light cream *or* milk
 Snipped parsley
 (optional)

Thaw fish and shrimp, if frozen. Devein shrimp, if necessary.

Drizzle each fillet with *some* of the lemon juice; sprinkle the fish with salt and pepper. Sprinkle *one side* of each fish fillet with *1 tablespoon* of the parsley. Roll up fish fillets, with parsley to the inside. Place the fish roll-ups, seam side down, in a 5x5x1½-inch baking dish. Cover and bake in a 425° oven for 10 minutes. Drain off cooking liquid.

Meanwhile, cook the shrimp in boiling water for 1 to 3 minutes or till shrimp turn pink.

For sauce, in a small saucepan stir the dry mustard into cornstarch. Add cream or milk all at once. Cook and stir till the mixture is thickened and bubbly. Cook and stir for 2 minutes more. Stir the shrimp into the thickened mixture; heat through.

Pour the shrimp sauce over the fish roll-ups. Bake, uncovered, for 10 minutes more. Sprinkle with additional parsley, if desired. Makes 2 servings.

*Note: If using canned shrimp, drain and rinse the shrimp.

Spring Aspic

1 envelope unflavored
 gelatin
1 13¾-ounce can chicken
 broth
1 small carrot, thinly sliced
 (⅓ cup)
 Dash onion powder
⅓ cup frozen peas
¼ cup sliced pitted ripe
 olives
 Bibb lettuce

Soften the gelatin in *¼ cup* of the broth; set aside. In a small saucepan cook the carrot slices, covered, in the remaining broth about 8 minutes or just till tender.

Remove the carrot slices with a slotted spoon; set aside. Add the gelatin mixture and onion powder to the broth in the saucepan. Cook and stir over low heat till the gelatin is dissolved. Remove from heat; add peas. Let stand 5 minutes. Stir in carrots and olives.

Pour the gelatin mixture into two 10-ounce custard cups or molds. Chill for several hours or till firm. To serve, invert aspics onto 2 lettuce-lined plates. Makes 2 servings.

● **Note:** To arrange vegetables in aspic, remove the peas from the saucepan with a slotted spoon after letting them stand for 5 minutes. Do not add carrots and olives. Spoon *1 tablespoon* of the gelatin mixture into *each* cup or mold. Chill till almost firm. Arrange olive slices around edge. Arrange the carrot slices in the center. Carefully spoon *3 more tablespoons* of the gelatin mixture into *each* cup. Chill till almost firm. Arrange peas atop. Spoon *5 more tablespoons* gelatin mixture into *each* cup. Pour the remaining gelatin mixture (about ½ cup mixture) into an ungreased 4½x2½x1½-inch loaf pan. Chill all till firm. Cut the aspic in the loaf pan into ¼-inch cubes. Unmold aspic cups as above and garnish with aspic cubes.

Raspberry Chantilly

1¼ cups fresh red raspberries, blackberries, *or*
 sliced strawberries
 or one 10-ounce pack-
 age frozen red rasp-
 berries, blackberries,
 or sliced strawberries
 (in quick-thaw pouch)
½ cup frozen whipped
 dessert topping,
 thawed
2 tablespoons dry *or*
 cream sherry

Clean the fresh berries. Crush enough berries to yield 3 tablespoons juice; discard crushed berries, reserving juice. Set 2 fresh berries aside for a garnish, if desired. (*Or,* thaw frozen berries according to the package directions. Drain berries, reserving 3 tablespoons juice.)

In a small mixing bowl place the dessert topping. Fold the reserved berry juice into topping.

To serve, spoon the berries into 2 dessert bowls. Drizzle *half* of the sherry over each. Spoon the topping mixture atop. Garnish with the reserved fresh berries, if desired. Makes 2 servings.

● **Peach Chantilly:** Prepare the Raspberry Chantilly as directed above, *except* omit the berries and sherry. Drain one 8¾-ounce can *peach slices,* chilled, reserving 3 tablespoons juice.

In a small mixing bowl fold the reserved juice and ¼ teaspoon *vanilla* into the dessert topping.

Serve as directed above. Garnish each serving with finely shredded *orange peel*, if desired. Makes 2 servings.

Deluxe Dinners

MENU

Bacon-Stuffed Steak Pinwheels

Steamed Broccoli

Fluted Mushrooms

Baked Potato with Sour Cream and Chives

Chocolate Bavarian

Three-Spice Coffee

Three-Spice Coffee

1½ cups water
¼ cup ground coffee
3 inches stick cinnamon, broken up
3 whole cloves
1 whole cardamom pod, cracked (optional)

Pour the *cold* water into a 6-cup percolator; stand the stem and basket firmly in the pot. In the basket combine the coffee, cinnamon, cloves, and cardamom, if desired. Replace the basket lid and cover the pot. Perk for 6 to 8 minutes. Makes 2 servings.

• **Drip coffee directions:** Make the coffee mixture in the coffee basket as directed above.

For *electric drip coffee makers,* pour the *cold* water into the upper compartment. Place the coffee pot on the heating element; allow the water to drip through the coffee mixture in the coffee basket.

For *non-electric drip coffee makers,* pour the *boiling* water over the coffee in basket. Simply allow the water to drip through the coffee basket into the bottom section. When the coffee has finished dripping, remove the basket and discard coffee grounds. Stir and serve. Keep warm over low heat.

Timetable

• **At least 4 hours** before serving, prepare Chocolate Bavarian and chill.
• **One hour** before serving, bake the potatoes.
• Prepare and bake the Bacon-Stuffed Steak Pinwheels.
• Steam broccoli.
• Flute mushrooms.
• Prepare Three-Spice Coffee.

Chocolate Bavarian

1 tablespoon sugar
1 square (1 ounce) semisweet chocolate, cut up
½ teaspoon unflavored gelatin
2 tablespoons milk
1 beaten egg yolk
1 teaspoon white crème de menthe (optional)
1 egg white
¼ cup frozen whipped dessert topping, thawed
Frozen whipped dessert topping, thawed

In a 1-quart saucepan combine the sugar, chocolate, and gelatin. Stir in the milk and egg yolk. Cook and stir over low heat till the chocolate is melted and mixture thickens slightly. Remove from heat. Stir in the crème de menthe, if desired. Chill till the mixture is the consistency of unbeaten egg whites (partially set), stirring frequently.

In a small mixer bowl beat the egg white till stiff peaks form (tips stand straight). Fold the beaten egg white into the chocolate mixture; fold in the ¼ cup whipped dessert topping. Turn the mixture into two 6-ounce molds. Cover and chill for 4 hours or till set.

To serve, unmold onto plates. Garnish with the additional dessert topping. Makes 2 servings.

Bacon-Stuffed Steak Pinwheels

4 slices bacon
¼ cup chopped fresh mushrooms
2 tablespoons chopped onion
2 tablespoons fine dry bread crumbs
2 tablespoons shredded Swiss cheese (½ ounce)
1 tablespoon snipped parsley
Dash pepper
½ pound beef top round steak, cut ¼ inch thick
1 tablespoon cooking oil
⅓ cup water

For stuffing, in a skillet cook the bacon just till tender; remove and drain on paper toweling. Reserve 1 tablespoon drippings in the skillet. Cook the mushrooms and onion in the reserved drippings till tender but not brown. Remove from heat; stir in bread crumbs, cheese, parsley, and pepper. Set aside.

Cut the steak into 4 strips, about 1 inch wide. Place 2 strips together, overlapping the ends, to form a long strip. Repeat with the remaining meat. Pound the strips to flatten slightly. Spread the stuffing atop the meat. Roll up jelly-roll style. With spiral side up, wrap 2 slices bacon around each meat roll-up; secure with wooden picks.

In a skillet brown the meat roll-ups on both sides in hot oil. Place in an 8x8x2-inch baking pan; add the water. Cover the pan with foil. Bake in a 350° oven about 45 minutes or till the meat is done. Makes 2 servings.

MENU

Fettuccine with Olives

Chicken Marsala

Breadsticks
Butter Curls or Molds

Creamy Orange Zabaglione

Sugar Cookies

White Wine

Espresso Coffee

Fettuccine with Olives

(pictured on pages 6 and 7)

1　ounce green *or* white
　　fettuccine, linguine, *or*
　　spaghetti (broken in
　　half)
2　tablespoons sliced
　　pitted ripe olives
3　cherry tomatoes, halved
1　tablespoon salad oil
1　tablespoon vinegar
¼　teaspoon dried basil,
　　crushed
¼　teaspoon sugar
　　Dash garlic salt
　　Dash onion salt
　　Dash bottled hot pepper
　　sauce

Cook pasta according to package directions; drain well. In a mixing bowl combine the pasta, olives, and tomatoes.

For dressing, in a screw-top jar combine salad oil, vinegar, basil, sugar, garlic salt, onion salt, and bottled hot pepper sauce. Cover and shake well to mix.

Pour the dressing over pasta mixture and toss to coat. Cover and chill for at least 3 hours or overnight, stirring the pasta mixture occasionally.

Before serving, toss gently to coat the pasta. Makes 2 servings.

Timetable

● **At least three hours** or the day before serving, prepare the Fettuccine with Olives and chill.
● Make butter curls or molds and chill.
● Chill the wine.
● **Up to one and one-half hours** before serving, prepare and chill custard for Creamy Orange Zabaglione.
● Prepare Chicken Marsala.
● Make espresso coffee.
● Whip cream and finish preparing Creamy Orange Zabaglione.

Creamy Orange Zabaglione

(pictured on pages 6 and 7)

2　egg yolks
1　tablespoon sugar
½　teaspoon finely
　　shredded orange peel
3　tablespoons orange
　　juice
1　tablespoon dry Marsala
　　(optional)
¼　cup whipping cream
　　Sliced almonds, toasted

In a heat-proof mixer bowl combine the egg yolks, sugar, orange peel, orange juice, and the Marsala, if desired. Beat with an electric mixer or wire whisk till frothy. Place the bowl over a saucepan of boiling water (water should not touch the bottom of bowl). Beat the mixture over the boiling water for 6 to 8 minutes or till mixture thickens and mounds.

When mixture is thick, place the bowl in a larger bowl of ice water; continue beating mixture for 2 to 3 minutes or till cool. Cover and chill for up to 1½ hours.

Before serving, beat the whipping cream till soft peaks form (tips curl over). Fold into chilled mixture. Spoon mixture into long-stemmed goblets. Top with sliced almonds. Makes 2 servings.

Chicken Marsala

(pictured on pages 6 and 7)

Marsala or dry sherry lends a delicate flavor to this Italian chicken dish—

1　medium chicken breast,
　　skinned, halved
　　lengthwise, and boned
1　tablespoon butter *or*
　　margarine
¾　cup sliced fresh
　　mushrooms
1　green onion, cut
　　into julienne strips
1　large carrot, cut into
　　julienne strips
1　stalk celery, cut into
　　julienne strips
¾　cup fresh *or* frozen
　　brussels sprouts,
　　halved
⅓　cup chicken broth
¼　cup dry Marsala *or* dry
　　sherry
2　whole fresh mushrooms,
　　fluted (optional)

In a 10-inch skillet quickly brown chicken breast halves in hot butter or margarine. Stir in the sliced mushrooms, green onion strips, carrot strips, celery strips, brussels sprout halves, chicken broth, and Marsala or sherry. Bring to boiling; reduce heat. Cover and simmer for 15 to 20 minutes or till chicken is done and vegetables are tender.

With a slotted spoon transfer the chicken and vegetables to a serving platter; reserve the cooking liquid. Garnish chicken with the fluted mushrooms, if desired. Cover and keep warm.

Bring the reserved cooking liquid in skillet to boiling. Cook, uncovered, till liquid is reduced to half the volume. Pour the reduced liquid atop the chicken and vegetables. Makes 2 servings.

Deluxe Dinners

MENU

Broiled Lobster Tails
with Orange Butter

———

Cauliflower Vinaigrette

———

Wild Rice

———

Mocha Coffee

Timetable

• **At least three hours** or the day before serving, prepare the Cauliflower Vinaigrette and chill.
• Partially thaw the lobster tails.
• **One hour** before serving, cook the wild rice.
• Prepare the lobster tails.
• Prepare the orange butter and broil the lobster.
• Make Mocha Coffee.

Broiled Lobster Tails with Orange Butter

2 6-ounce frozen lobster
    tails
2 tablespoons butter *or*
    margarine, melted
1 tablespoon orange juice
    Dash salt
    Snipped parsley
    Orange wedges
    (optional)

Partially thaw the lobster tails. Use a sharp, heavy knife to cut down center of the hard top shell. Cut through meat, but not through the undershell. Spread the tails open butterfly-style so the lobster meat is on top. Place the lobster tails, shell side down, on rack of an unheated broiler pan.

Combine the melted butter or margarine, the orange juice, and salt; brush over lobster. Broil the lobster 4 inches from heat for 14 to 15 minutes or till the lobster meat loses its translucency and flakes easily when tested with a fork; brush with butter mixture once during broiling.

Loosen meat from shell by inserting a fork between the shell and meat. Brush the lobster with the remaining butter mixture before serving; garnish with parsley. Serve with orange wedges, if desired. Makes 2 servings.

Cauliflower Vinaigrette

1½ cups fresh *or* frozen
     cauliflower flowerets
¼   cup salad oil
2   tablespoons vinegar
1   tablespoon sugar
½   teaspoon curry powder
⅛   teaspoon pepper
2   tablespoons sliced
    pimiento, drained
2   tablespoons sliced
    green onion
    Lettuce leaves

In a saucepan cook fresh cauliflower in a small amount of boiling salted water about 10 minutes or till crisp-tender. (Or, cook frozen cauliflower according to the package directions). Drain.

For dressing, in a screw-top jar combine the salad oil, vinegar, sugar, curry powder, and pepper. Cover and shake well to mix.

Place the cauliflower, pimiento, and green onion in a mixing bowl. Pour dressing over all. Cover and chill at least three hours or overnight, spooning the dressing over vegetables occasionally.

To serve, with a slotted spoon lift vegetables from dressing. Arrange the vegetables on 2 individual lettuce-lined salad plates. Spoon some of the dressing over vegetables. Pass the remaining dressing. Makes 2 servings.

Mocha Coffee

1 cup hot strong
   coffee (8 ounces)
2 tablespoons light cream
2 tablespoons crème de
   cacao
   Pressurized dessert
   topping *or* whipped
   cream
   Grated *or* shaved
   chocolate

In a 2-cup glass measure or in a heat-proof pitcher combine the hot strong coffee, the 2 tablespoons light cream, and crème de cacao. Pour into 2 coffee cups or mugs. Garnish each cup of coffee with the pressurized dessert topping or whipped cream and the grated or shaved chocolate (see tip on page 86). Makes 2 (6-ounce) servings.
• **Double Coffee:** Prepare Mocha Coffee as directed above, *except* substitute 1 tablespoon *coffee liqueur* for 1 tablespoon of crème de cacao. Garnish as above.
• **Chocolate-Mint Coffee:** Make Mocha Coffee as directed above, *except* substitute 1 tablespoon of *chocolate-mint liqueur* for crème de cacao. Garnish as directed in recipe above. Serve with *peppermint stick stirrers,* if desired.
• **Café Orange:** Prepare Mocha Coffee as directed above, *except* substitute 1 tablespoon *orange liqueur* for crème de cacao. Garnish topping with finely shredded *orange peel* instead of chocolate.
• **Coffee Amandine:** Make the Mocha Coffee as directed above, *except* substitute 2 tablespoons *Amaretto* for the crème de cacao. Garnish the whipped dessert topping with some toasted, slivered *almonds* instead of chocolate.

MENU

Gazpacho Soufflé

Artichokes with
Shallot Sauce

Crescent Rolls

Coeurs à la Crème

Coffee or Tea

Timetable

• **At least three hours** or the day before serving, make the Coeurs à la Crème and sauce.
• **About 50 minutes** before serving, bake crescent rolls.
• Prepare Gazpacho Soufflé.
• Cook Artichokes with Shallot Sauce.
• Make coffee or tea.
• Unmold Coeurs à la Crème.

Gazpacho Soufflé

2 tablespoons chopped onion
2 tablespoons chopped green pepper
2 tablespoons butter *or* margarine
2 tablespoons all-purpose flour
Dash garlic powder
Dash pepper
Dash bottled hot pepper sauce
½ of an 8-ounce can tomato sauce (½ cup)
2 egg yolks
½ cup diced fully cooked ham
2 tablespoons chopped pimiento
2 egg whites

Cook onion and green pepper in hot butter till tender. Stir in flour, garlic powder, pepper, and hot pepper sauce. Add tomato sauce. Cook and stir till thickened and bubbly. Cook and stir for 1 minute more. Remove from heat.

Beat egg yolks about 5 minutes. Gradually stir hot mixture into egg yolks. Stir in ham and pimiento.

Using clean beaters, beat egg whites till stiff peaks form. Fold tomato mixture into egg whites. Turn into a 3-cup ungreased soufflé dish. Bake in a 350° oven 30 to 35 minutes or till a knife inserted near center comes out clean. Serve immediately. Makes 2 servings.

Coeurs à la Crème

These French desserts are made in heart-shaped molds—

2 6-inch squares of cheesecloth, moistened
1 3-ounce package cream cheese, softened
Several drops almond extract
2 tablespoons powdered sugar
⅓ cup frozen whipped dessert topping, thawed
2 tablespoons strawberry preserves
1 tablespoon dry white wine

Line two 3-inch *coeur à la crème* molds or ½-cup molds with the cheesecloth squares, allowing the cheesecloth edges to overhang. In a small mixer bowl beat together the cream cheese and the almond extract. Gradually add the sugar, beating on high speed of electric mixer till light and fluffy.

Fold the topping into the cream cheese mixture. Spoon the mixture into molds. Cover and chill for at least 3 hours or overnight.

For sauce, stir together the preserves and wine. Cover and chill.

Before serving, invert the molds onto two dessert plates. Peel off cheesecloth. Spoon the sauce over top. Makes 2 servings.

Artichokes with Shallot Sauce

2 artichokes
2 tablespoons chopped shallots *or* sliced green onion
1 tablespoon butter *or* margarine
½ cup chicken broth
1½ teaspoons cornstarch
1½ teaspoons lemon juice
Dash dried rosemary, crushed

Remove stems and loose outer leaves from artichokes. Cut 1 inch from tops; snip off sharp leaf tips. Cook artichokes in boiling salted water for 20 to 30 minutes or till outer leaves come out with a slight pull. Drain upside down.

Meanwhile, for sauce, in a skillet cook the shallots or green onion in hot butter or margarine till tender but not brown. Combine chicken broth, cornstarch, lemon juice, and rosemary. Stir into skillet. Cook and stir till thickened and bubbly. Cook and stir for 2 minutes more. Serve the sauce with artichokes. Makes 2 servings.

• **Microwave directions:** Trim the artichokes as directed above. Place artichokes in an 8x8x2-inch baking dish. Pour in water to a depth of ¼ inch. Cover dish with vented plastic wrap. Cook in a counter-top microwave oven on high power for 9 to 15 minutes or till the artichokes are done, rotating dish a half-turn after half the cooking time.

In a 2-cup glass measure combine the butter or margarine and shallots or green onion. Micro-cook, covered with waxed paper, on high power for 1½ minutes or till tender.

Combine chicken broth, cornstarch, lemon juice, and rosemary; add to the measuring cup. Micro-cook, covered, 1 minute. Remove and stir. Return to oven; cook 1½ to 2 minutes more, stirring every 30 seconds. Serve artichokes with the shallot sauce.

Simple-to-Fix Suppers

MENU

Pork Chops with Mushroom Gravy

Zucchini-Carrot Sauté

Mashed Potatoes with Fines Herbes

Hard Rolls

Strawberry Meringue Puffs

Coffee or Tea

These simple-to-fix suppers are meant for those days when you want some easy, flavorful home cooking.

The following menus illustrate the variety of dishes you can create by using fairly common ingredients. In fact, you should have most of them on hand. But just to be sure, check your cupboards and refrigerator. Jot down any staple items you may need to replace along with any additional ingredients you require.

Once you've collected all of the ingredients for several of these menus, you can choose which one you want to eat right before you start to cook it, without running to the store.

When you do fix supper, have some fun and speed up food preparation at the same time. Try cooking together in the kitchen. You can each prepare a complete recipe from the menu or just divide the steps in the timetable between you. Then the two of you can sit down to a home-cooked meal that you'll both be proud of.

Timetable

• **About one hour** before serving, prepare the meringue puffs for the dessert and cool to room temperature.

• Cook pork chops, mushrooms, and onion in a skillet. Cover and simmer the pork chop mixture.

• Boil the potatoes for Mashed Potatoes with Fines Herbes.

• Prepare either the Zucchini-Carrot Sauté or Steamed Zucchini and Carrots. Keep vegetables warm.

• Finish making Mashed Potatoes with Fines Herbes and broil.

• Make coffee or tea.

• Make the mushroom gravy for the pork chops.

• Finish preparing the Strawberry Meringue Puffs before serving.

Mashed Potatoes with Fines Herbes

(pictured on the cover)

2 medium potatoes,
    peeled and cut up
2 tablespoons dairy sour
    cream
¼ teaspoon salt
    Dash pepper
    Dash fines herbes

Cook the potatoes in boiling salted water about 20 minutes or till tender; drain. Transfer the potatoes to a small mixer bowl; add the sour cream, salt, pepper, and fines herbes. Beat on medium speed of electric mixer till the potato mixture is smooth.

Using a pastry bag fitted with a large star tip, pipe the potato mixture into 2 mounds on greased heavy-duty foil on a baking sheet. (*Or*, spoon the potato mixture into two mounds). Broil the potato mounds 5 inches from heat about 5 minutes or till light brown. Makes 2 servings.

Zucchini-Carrot Sauté

(pictured on the cover)

If you want to eliminate some of the last-minute preparation or cut a few calories, make Steamed Zucchini and Carrots instead of the Zucchini-Carrot Sauté—

- 1 medium carrot, cut into julienne strips
- ½ medium zucchini, cut into julienne strips
- 1 tablespoon butter *or* margarine
- 1 tablespoon Italian salad dressing
- ½ teaspoon sesame seed
  Dash bottled hot pepper sauce

In a small saucepan cook carrot strips in boiling salted water for 5 to 7 minutes or till crisp-tender; drain.

In a medium skillet cook zucchini strips and carrot strips in hot butter or margarine till the zucchini is tender but not brown. Stir in the Italian salad dressing, the sesame seed, and the bottled hot pepper sauce. Heat through, gently tossing the vegetables to coat. Makes 2 servings.

● **Steamed Zucchini and Carrots:** Cut carrots and zucchini as directed in Zucchini-Carrot Sauté. Omit the remaining ingredients. Place the carrot strips in a steamer basket. Place the basket over boiling water. Cover and steam for 10 minutes. Add the zucchini strips. Cover and steam the vegetables for 10 minutes more.

Pork Chops with Mushroom Gravy

(pictured on the cover)

- 2 pork loin chops, cut ½ inch thick (about 1½ pounds)
- 1 tablespoon cooking oil
  Salt
  Pepper
- ½ cup sliced fresh mushrooms
- 2 tablespoons chopped onion
- ½ cup chicken broth
- 1 teaspoon dry sherry (optional)
- ¼ teaspoon dried thyme, crushed
- ⅛ teaspoon salt
- 2 tablespoons cold water
- 1 tablespoon all-purpose flour
- 1 tablespoon snipped chives
  Chives (optional)

In a 10-inch skillet brown pork chops on both sides in hot cooking oil. Remove and sprinkle the chops with salt and pepper; set aside. Add mushrooms and onion to drippings in skillet and cook till onion is tender but not brown. Add chicken broth; sherry, if desired; thyme; the ⅛ teaspoon salt; and the chops to the skillet. Cover and simmer the meat for 35 to 40 minutes. Transfer the chops to a serving platter, reserving juices; keep the chops warm.

For mushroom gravy, spoon fat from juices. Add water, if necessary, to the juices to measure ½ cup liquid. Combine the 2 tablespoons cold water and flour. Stir into the juices in skillet; add the 1 tablespoon snipped chives. Cook and stir till thickened and bubbly. Cook and stir for 1 minute more. Spoon some of the gravy over the pork chops and sprinkle with additional snipped chives, if desired. Pass the remaining gravy. Garnish with the whole chives, if desired. Makes 2 servings.

Strawberry Meringue Puffs

(pictured on the cover)

Try substituting different kinds of berries and ice cream flavors for the strawberries and strawberry ice cream the next time you make this luscious, light dessert—

- ½ cup sliced fresh strawberries *or* ½ of a 10-ounce package frozen sliced strawberries *or* ½ of a 16-ounce can strawberries, sliced
- 1 egg white
- ¼ teaspoon vanilla
- ¼ cup sugar
- 2 cake dessert cups
- 2 scoops strawberry ice cream

Clean fresh berrries. (*Or,* thaw the frozen berries. Drain thawed or canned berries).

For meringue, in a mixer bowl beat egg white and vanilla on medium speed of electric mixer till soft peaks form (tips curl over). Gradually add the sugar, beating till stiff peaks form (tips stand straight).

Spread the meringue on the top and sides of the cake dessert cups. Place the meringue-coated cups on lightly greased baking sheet. Bake in a 450° oven for 4 to 5 minutes or till golden. Cool to room temperature.

Before serving, fill the center of each meringue cup with a scoop of the strawberry ice cream. Spoon sliced strawberries over the ice cream. Makes 2 servings.

Simple-to-Fix Suppers

Lemon-Parsley Potatoes

    6 tiny new potatoes *or*
       2 medium potatoes
    2 tablespoons butter *or*
       margarine
    2 teaspoons lemon juice
    ⅛ teaspoon salt
    1 tablespoon snipped
       parsley

Scrub the new potatoes. If desired, with a vegetable peeler remove narrow strip of peel around the centers of new potatoes. (*Or,* peel and quarter medium potatoes.)

In a medium saucepan cook the potatoes in boiling salted water about 20 minutes or till tender. Drain.

In an 8-inch skillet melt the butter or margarine. Add the lemon juice and salt. Stir till well combined. Add the potatoes. Cook and stir over low heat about 7 minutes or till the potatoes are well-coated. Add the snipped parsley and toss lightly. Makes 2 servings.

Timetable

● **At least 4 hours** or the day before serving, prepare Berry-Buttermilk Bisque. Cover the soup and chill.
● **One and one-half hours** before serving, cook Scandinavian Short Ribs.
● **Thirty minutes** before serving, prepare Lemon-Parsley Potatoes.
● Cook carrot slices and toss with fresh or dried dill.
● Make coffee or tea.
● Thicken the sauce for the ribs.

Berry-Buttermilk Bisque

    ⅔ cup fresh *or* frozen
       unsweetened raspber-
       ries, strawberries, *or*
       blueberries
    ½ cup water
    2 tablespoons sugar
    ¼ teaspoon grated orange
       peel
    1 tablespoon orange juice
    ⅔ cup buttermilk
       Mint leaf (optional)

Clean the fresh berries. (*Or,* thaw and drain frozen berrries). Slice the strawberries. If desired, reserve two berries for garnish.

In a 1-quart saucepan combine the fresh or thawed berries, the water, sugar, orange peel, and orange juice. Bring the mixture to boiling, stirring occasionally; reduce heat. Cover and simmer for 10 minutes. Remove the saucepan from heat; let the mixture cool for 30 minutes.

Pour the cooled berry mixture into blender container. Cover and blend till the mixture is smooth. Add the buttermilk. Cover and blend till well combined. Cover and chill for at least 3 hours. Garnish each serving with one of the reserved berries and a mint leaf, if desired. Makes 2 servings.

Scandinavian Short Ribs

    ¼ cup chopped onion
    1 tablespoon butter *or*
       margarine
    1 5½-ounce can apple
       cider *or* apple juice
    2 teaspoons catsup
    ⅛ teaspoon salt
    ⅛ teaspoon dried basil,
       crushed
       Dash ground allspice
       Dash ground cloves
    4 beef short ribs, cut into
       serving-size pieces
       (about 1 pound)
    1 tablespoon water
    2 teaspoons cornstarch
    2 teaspoons pickle relish
       (optional)

In a medium saucepan cook the onion in hot butter or margarine till tender but not brown. Stir in the apple cider or juice, catsup, salt, basil, allspice, and cloves. Trim the fat from ribs; add the ribs to saucepan. Bring to boiling; reduce heat. Cover and simmer for 1¼ to 1½ hours or till meat is tender. Transfer ribs to a serving platter, reserving cooking liquid; keep the ribs warm.

For sauce, skim fat from cooking liquid. Measure cooking liquid; add water, if necessary, to make ⅔ cup. Stir together the 1 tablespoon water and the cornstarch; stir into cooking liquid. Cook and stir till the mixture is thickened and bubbly. Cook and stir for 2 minutes more. Stir in the pickle relish, if desired. Spoon some of the sauce over the ribs. Pass remaining sauce. Makes 2 servings.

MENU

Veal Schnitzel

Green Salad with Zesty Dressing

Noodles with Parsley

Dark Rye Bread Butter or Margarine

Honey-Fruit Compote

Milk

Green Salad with Zesty Dressing

2 **cups torn salad greens**
1 **medium tomato, cut into wedges**
¼ **cup chopped celery**
1 **teaspoon snipped chives** *or* **sliced green onion**
   Zesty Dressing

Prepare and chill Zesty Dressing. In a salad bowl combine the torn salad greens, tomato wedges, chopped celery, and chives. Pour the chilled dressing over salad; toss lightly to coat the vegetables. Makes 2 servings.

• **Zesty Dressing:** In a screw-top jar combine 2 tablespoons *white wine vinegar*, 2 tablespoons *salad oil*, 1 tablespoon *sugar*, ¼ teaspoon *dry mustard*, a few drops of *Worcestershire sauce*, dash *salt*, a dash *onion powder*, and a dash *bottled hot pepper sauce*. Cover the jar tightly and shake to mix the dressing well. Chill for at least 3 hours.* Shake the dressing again before serving. Makes ⅓ cup dressing.

*Note: You can make a double quantity of dressing and store it, tightly covered, in the refrigerator for up to one month.

Timetable

• **At least three hours** before serving, make Honey-Fruit Compote; cover and chill, if serving the compote cold.
• Make the dressing; cover and chill.
• **Forty minutes** before serving, make the Honey-Fruit Compote, if serving warm.
• Meanwhile, prepare and toss the salad; cover and chill.
• Pound and coat the meat.
• Cook the meat and keep warm.
• Meanwhile, cook the noodles and toss with snipped parsley.
• Prepare the gravy for the meat.
• Pour the dressing over salad and toss.

Honey-Fruit Compote

1 **cup mixed dried fruit**
½ **cup orange juice**
1 **tablespoon honey**
¼ **teaspoon ground cinnamon**
   Dash ground nutmeg
2 **teaspoons orange liqueur**

In a small saucepan combine the dried fruit, orange juice, honey, cinnamon, and nutmeg. Bring to boiling; reduce heat. Cover and simmer for 15 to 20 minutes or till the fruit is tender. Remove the saucepan from heat. Stir in the orange liqueur. Spoon the mixture into 2 individual dessert dishes. Serve the compote warm or chilled. Makes 2 servings.

Veal Schnitzel

½ **pound veal** *or* **beef round steak**
1 **tablespoon all-purpose flour**
   Salt
   Pepper
1 **beaten egg**
2 **tablespoons milk**
⅓ **cup fine dry bread crumbs**
2 **tablespoons cooking oil**
½ **cup water**
3 **tablespoons dairy sour cream**
1 **tablespoon all-purpose flour**
1 **lemon, sliced (optional)**

Cut the veal or beef steak into 2 serving-size portions; place *each* portion between 2 pieces of clear plastic wrap. Pound the meat with a meat mallet to ¼- to ⅛-inch thickness, working from center to edges. Cut small slits around the edges to prevent curling.

Coat the meat with 1 tablespoon flour; sprinkle with salt and pepper. Combine the egg and milk. Dip the meat into the egg mixture and then into bread crumbs to coat evenly.

In a 10-inch skillet cook the meat in hot cooking oil for 3 to 5 minutes on each side or till tender and brown. Transfer the meat to dinner plates; keep warm.

For gravy, add the water to the skillet; stir to loosen the brown pieces from the skillet. In a small mixing bowl combine sour cream and 1 tablespoon flour. Stir *some* of the cooking liquid into the sour cream mixture. Return all to skillet. Cook and stir till the mixture is thickened and bubbly. Cook and stir for 1 minute more. Season to taste with salt and pepper.

Spoon some of the gravy over the meat. Garnish with lemon slices, if desired. Pass the remaining gravy. Makes 2 servings.

Simple-to-Fix Suppers

MENU

Walnut-Chicken Curry

Hot Cooked Rice

Chutney Tossed Salad

Pita Bread Rounds

Cranberry-Orange Slush or Cranberry-Orange Cooler

Cranberry-Orange Slush

1 **11-ounce can mandarin orange sections (packed in pineapple juice)**
½ **cup cranberry juice cocktail**
½ **cup lemon-lime carbonated beverage**

In blender container combine the *undrained* oranges and cranberry juice cocktail. Cover and blend till frothy. Pour the mixture into a 7x5x3-inch loaf pan. Freeze till the mixture is firm.

Remove the loaf pan from the freezer and let the frozen mixture stand for 10 to 15 minutes.

To make slush, scrape a spoon across the surface of the frozen orange mixture; spoon into a mixing bowl. Gradually add the carbonated beverage, stirring gently to combine. Spoon the slush mixture into 2 tall glasses. Makes 2 (12-ounce) servings.

• **Cranberry-Orange Cooler:** In a blender container prepare Cranberry-Orange Slush as directed above, *except* do not freeze the mixture. Pour the mixture over *ice cubes* in tall glasses. Makes 2 (12-ounce) servings.

Timetable

• **At least 6 hours** or the day before serving, prepare mixture for the slush and freeze.
• Make the salad dressing; cover and chill.
• **One hour** before serving, prepare Walnut-Chicken Curry.
• Meanwhile, cut up and toss together the ingredients for salad; cover and chill.
• Remove the slush mixture from freezer and let stand.
• Cook rice.
• Finish preparing Cranberry-Orange Slush or prepare Cranberry-Orange Cooler.

Chutney Tossed Salad

1 **tablespoon white wine vinegar**
1 **tablespoon salad oil**
1 **tablespoon chopped chutney**
½ **teaspoon sugar**
⅛ **teaspoon salt**
¼ **teaspoon dry mustard**
2 **cups torn salad greens**
½ **cup chopped apple**
1 **stalk celery, sliced**
3 **tablespoons light raisins**
1 **tablespoon sliced green onion**
Lettuce leaves (optional)

For dressing, in a screw-top jar combine vinegar, salad oil, chutney, sugar, salt, and mustard. Cover the jar tightly and shake well to mix; chill.

Before serving, in a salad bowl combine the torn salad greens, apple, celery, raisins, and green onion. Shake the dressing again; pour over the salad and toss lightly to coat. If desired, serve the salad in 2 individual lettuce-lined salad bowls. Makes 2 servings.

Walnut-Chicken Curry

4 **chicken drumsticks** *or* **chicken thighs** *or* **2 chicken legs** *or* **1 whole medium chicken breast, halved lengthwise**
1 **tablespoon cooking oil**
2 **tablespoons chopped onion**
1 **clove garlic, minced**
1 **to 2 teaspoons curry powder**
⅓ **cup water**
2 **tablespoons catsup**
¼ **teaspoon salt**
⅛ **teaspoon ground cloves**
Dash pepper
½ **cup plain yogurt**
1 **tablespoon all-purpose flour**
2 **tablespoons chopped walnuts**
Hot cooked rice

In a medium skillet cook chicken pieces in hot cooking oil about 15 minutes or till brown. Remove the chicken, reserving drippings in the skillet. Cook the onion, garlic, and the curry powder in the reserved drippings till onion is tender but not brown. Remove from heat.

Stir water, catsup, salt, cloves, and pepper into the curry mixture. Return the chicken pieces to the skillet. Bring to boiling; reduce heat. Cover and simmer for 30 to 35 minutes or till the chicken is tender. Remove the chicken and set aside.

Stir together the yogurt and the flour; stir into the hot curry mixture. Cook and stir till the mixture is thickened and bubbly. Cook and stir for 2 minutes more. Stir in the chopped walnuts and the chicken. Heat through. Serve over the hot cooked rice. Makes 2 servings.

MENU

**Green Bean and
Fish Amandine**

**Herb-Sour Cream Dip
with Vegetable Dippers**

**Dinner Rolls
Butter or Margarine**

**Brandied Peaches
'n' Ice Cream**

Beverage

Sour Cream-Herb Dip

⅓ cup sour cream dip with chives
½ teaspoon Worcestershire sauce
¼ teaspoon Italian seasoning
Dash onion powder or garlic powder
Assorted vegetable dippers*

In a small mixing bowl stir together the sour cream dip with chives, the Worcestershire sauce, Italian seasoning, and onion powder or garlic powder. Cover and chill till serving time.

Serve the chilled sour cream dip with assorted vegetable dippers.* Makes about ⅓ cup dip.

*Note: For dippers, choose from the following fresh vegetable options: sliced mushrooms, cucumber, or zucchini; carrot or celery sticks; avocado or green pepper strips; broccoli buds or cauliflower flowerets, and radishes or brussels sprout halves.

Timetable

• **Two hours** or the day before serving, prepare the ice cream mixture for the dessert; freeze.
• Cut up the vegetables for dipping; cover and chill.
• Prepare Herb-Sour Cream Dip; cover and chill.
• **Twenty minutes** before serving, cook the fish and the green beans.
• Heat rolls, if desired.
• Prepare the sauce for fish.
• Prepare Brandied Peaches 'n' Ice Cream.

Brandied Peaches 'n' Ice Cream

1½ cups vanilla ice cream
2 tablespoons peach brandy or apricot brandy
1 8¾-ounce can peach slices or unpeeled apricot halves, drained
¼ cup frozen blueberries or other frozen berries, thawed and drained

In a chilled mixing bowl, stir the ice cream to soften. Quickly stir in the peach brandy or apricot brandy. Spoon *half* of the ice cream mixture into 2 brandy snifters or dessert bowls. Place the brandy snifters and remaining ice cream mixture in freezer (mixture will not freeze firm).

Before serving, spoon drained peach slices or apricot halves and thawed berries atop the ice cream mixture in the brandy snifters or bowls. Reserve 2 pieces of fruit for a garnish, if desired. Top with the remaining ice cream mixture. Garnish each with the reserved fruit, if desired. Makes 2 servings.

Green Bean and Fish Amandine

8 ounces fresh or frozen fish fillets
Water
1 tablespoon lemon juice
½ teaspoon salt
½ of a 9-ounce package frozen French-style green beans
⅔ cup milk
1 ounce process Swiss cheese, cut up (¼ cup)
1 tablespoon all-purpose flour
1 tablespoon butter or margarine
⅛ teaspoon salt
1 tablespoon dry sherry
Sliced almonds, toasted

Place fresh or frozen fish fillets in a 10-inch skillet. Add enough water to cover the fillets. Add the lemon juice and the ½ teaspoon salt. Bring to boiling; reduce heat. Cover and simmer fish about 12 minutes or till fish flakes easily when tested with a fork.

Meanwhile, cook green beans according to package directions; drain thoroughly.

For sauce, place milk, cheese, flour, butter or margarine, and ⅛ teaspoon salt in blender container. Cover and blend till the ingredients are combined. Pour the mixture into a saucepan. Cook and stir till the mixture is thickened and bubbly. Cook and stir for 1 minute more. Stir in the dry sherry and drained beans.

Drain the fish fillets and place on a platter. Spoon the green bean sauce over fish; sprinkle with almonds. Makes 2 servings.

Simple-to-Fix Suppers

MENU

Egg Foo Yung Casserole
with Chinese Brown Sauce

Teriyaki Spinach Salad

Coconut-Almond
Butter Cookies
or Fortune Cookies

Hot Tea

Timetable

- **At least three hours** or the day before serving, bake the Coconut-Almond Butter Cookies.
- Prepare Teriyaki Spinach Salad; cover and chill.
- **About 45 minutes** before serving, prepare the casserole and bake.
- Make the sauce.
- Make tea.

Coconut-Almond Butter Cookies

- ¼ cup butter or margarine
- ¼ cup sifted powdered sugar
- ⅛ teaspoon almond extract
- ½ cup all-purpose flour
- ¼ cup coconut
- 3 tablespoons ground almonds
- 1 tablespoon powdered sugar
- ⅛ teaspoon ground cinnamon

Let the butter or margarine stand at room temperature till softened. In a mixing bowl with the back of a wooden spoon cream the butter or margarine and the ¼ cup sugar together till fluffy. Stir in the almond extract. Stir in the flour till well combined. Stir in the coconut and ground almonds.

Shape the dough into 1-inch balls. Place the balls 2 inches apart on an ungreased cookie sheet. Bake in a 375° oven for 8 to 10 minutes. Place on a wire rack over waxed paper.

For topping, combine the 1 tablespoon powdered sugar and the cinnamon; sprinkle over the warm cookies. Cool thoroughly. Makes about 1½ dozen cookies.

Teriyaki Spinach Salad

- 1 tablespoon salad oil
- 1 tablespoon teriyaki sauce
- 1½ teaspoons lime juice
- 2 cups fresh spinach
- 1 medium zucchini, bias-sliced (1 cup)
- ¼ cup bamboo shoots, drained

For dressing, in a screw-top jar combine the salad oil, the teriyaki sauce and lime juice. Cover the jar tightly and shake to mix the dressing well; set aside.

Wash the spinach; pat dry with paper toweling. Remove the spinach stems and cut into 1-inch pieces. Tear the spinach leaves into bite-sized pieces.

In a salad bowl combine the torn spinach, zucchini slices, and bamboo shoots. Pour teriyaki dressing over the vegetables; toss lightly to coat. Cover the salad and chill at least 3 hours or overnight. Toss the salad again just before serving. Makes 2 servings.

Egg Foo Yung Casserole with Chinese Brown Sauce

- 2 tablespoons sliced green onion
- 2 tablespoons chopped celery
- 2 tablespoons chopped green pepper
- 1 tablespoon butter *or* margarine
- ½ cup canned bean sprouts, drained
  Dash salt
- 4 beaten eggs
  Chinese Brown Sauce

In a medium saucepan cook the green onion, celery, and green pepper in hot butter or margarine about 1 minute or just till crisp-tender. Remove from heat. Stir in the bean sprouts and salt. Add the vegetable mixture to the beaten eggs.

Place two 10-ounce greased individual casseroles or two 10-ounce greased custard cups in a 9x9x2-inch baking pan on oven rack. Pour the egg mixture into casseroles or custard cups. Pour boiling water into the pan around the casseroles or custard cups to a depth of 1 inch. Bake in a 350° oven for 25 to 30 minutes or till a knife inserted near the centers comes out clean.

Meanwhile, prepare the Chinese Brown Sauce. Spoon the warm sauce over each serving. Makes 2 servings.

- **Chinese Brown Sauce:** In a saucepan melt 1 tablespoon *butter or margarine*. Stir 1 teaspoon *cornstarch* and ½ teaspoon *sugar* into butter or margarine. Add ¼ cup *water* and 2 teaspoons *soy sauce* all at once. Cook and stir till the mixture is thickened and bubbly. Cook and stir the sauce for 2 minutes more.

MENU

Cheesy Walnut
Fettuccine

French Bread with
Parsley Butter

Yogurt-Melon
Sundaes

Beverage

French Bread with Parsley Butter

3 tablespoons butter *or* margarine
1½ teaspoons snipped fresh parsley *or* ½ teaspoon dried parsley flakes
½ teaspoon lemon juice
Dash pepper
4 1-inch slices French bread

To soften the butter or margarine,* cut into pieces; place in a heat-proof bowl in a cool oven. Turn the oven to 350°; heat for 3 minutes. Transfer the butter or margarine to a cool bowl to prevent melting.

Stir the fresh or dried parsley, the lemon juice, and pepper into the softened butter or margarine. Spread the parsley butter on the slices of French bread. Wrap the bread slices loosely in foil. Place in a 350° oven about 10 minutes or till the bread is heated through. Makes 2 servings.

*Note: Small amounts of butter or margarine can be softened by beating with a wooden spoon or an electric mixer.

Timetable

• **About 40 minutes** before serving, prepare Yogurt-Melon Sundaes and chill in the freezer till serving time.
• Cook the vegetables for Cheesy Walnut Fettuccine and drain.
• Prepare and spread the butter on the bread slices; wrap in foil.
• Cook the pasta and drain.
• Meanwhile, heat French bread slices.
• Make the vegetable sauce.
• Toss together the pasta and vegetable sauce.

Yogurt-Melon Sundaes

You can make melon balls with a teaspoon or melon baller instead of melon pieces if you'd like—

½ cup fresh *or* frozen sliced strawberries *or* red raspberries
1 cup cubed cantaloupe, honeydew melon, *or* other melon
⅔ cup peach, lemon, *or* pineapple frozen yogurt
Toasted coconut

Clean the fresh berries. (*Or,* thaw the frozen berries). Spoon the melon pieces into 2 sherbet dishes or dessert bowls. Spoon the peach, lemon, or pineapple frozen yogurt atop melon pieces. Top with the sliced strawberries or raspberries. Sprinkle with the toasted coconut. Chill the sundaes in the freezer till serving time. Makes 2 servings.

Cheesy Walnut Fettuccine

If you substitute cauliflower for the broccoli, add some color by using green noodles—

1 10-ounce package frozen cut broccoli *or* cauliflower
3 ounces fettuccine *or* spaghetti
1 tablespoon butter *or* margarine
1½ teaspoons all-purpose flour
1½ teaspoons snipped fresh basil *or* ½ teaspoon dried basil, crushed
Dash garlic powder
¾ cup milk *or* light cream
⅔ cup cream-style cottage cheese
¼ cup grated Parmesan cheese
¼ cup chopped walnuts *or* pecans
1 tablespoon butter *or* margarine

In a medium saucepan cook the broccoli or cauliflower according to package directions; drain. (If using frozen cauliflower, cut up any large pieces.) Cook the pasta according to the package directions; drain.

Meanwhile, for sauce, in medium saucepan melt 1 tablespoon butter or margarine. Stir in flour, basil, and garlic powder. Add milk or light cream all at once. Cook and stir till thickened and bubbly. Cook and stir for 1 minute more. Remove from heat; stir in the cottage cheese and the Parmesan cheese. Add the broccoli or cauliflower and walnuts or pecans; heat through, stirring occasionally.

Toss the cooked pasta with 1 tablespoon butter or margarine. Spoon the vegetable sauce over pasta. Toss to coat pasta. Pass additional Parmesan cheese, if desired. Makes 2 servings.

Beat-the-Clock Menus

MENU

**Steak in Lime Sauce
or Steak Piccata**

Buttered Green Beans

Spanish Rice

**Rainbow Sherbet Parfaits
or
Chocolate Ribbon Parfaits**

Spiced Mocha Coffee

When your schedule doesn't allow much time for meals, beat the clock by preparing one of these quick menus. From start to finish, each complete menu takes less than 45 minutes to prepare.

Save time by taking the time to read through each recipe. Then assemble your equipment and ingredients. Learn to dovetail the steps of recipes. For example, while the stew is simmering, toss the salad and heat the bread.

Though we've based all the preparation timings in this section on conventional cooking equipment and methods, you can use your timesaving appliances when possible. Process chopped ingredients in the blender or the food processor and rely on your microwave oven or your pressure cooker for precooking steps.

Shorten food preparation time by organizing your kitchen utensils according to use. Store all cookware by the range, storage containers near the refrigerator, and mixing equipment close to your largest work surface.

Timetable

*Total preparation time:
40 minutes*

• **Forty minutes** before serving, prepare Rainbow Sherbert Parfaits and freeze or prepare Chocolate Ribbon Parfaits and chill in the refrigerator.
• Cook bacon and crumble.
• Boil or steam fresh, canned, or frozen green beans.
• Prepare Spanish Rice.
• Prepare Steak in Lime Sauce or Steak Piccata.
• Make Spiced Mocha Coffee.
• Drain beans and stir in a tablespoon of butter or margarine.

Spiced Mocha Coffee

Assembling time: 5 minutes

    2 **teaspoons instant coffee
       crystals**
    1 **teaspoon presweetened
       cocoa powder**
       Dash ground cinnamon
  1½   **cups boiling water**
    ¼ **cup light cream *or* milk**
    2 **cinnamon sticks
       (optional)**

Combine the instant coffee crystals, cocoa powder, and ground cinnamon. Stir the boiling water into the coffee mixture. Stir in light cream or milk.

Pour coffee into 2 coffee cups or mugs. Serve each with a cinnamon stick stirrer, if desired. Makes 2 servings.

Spanish Rice

Cooking time: 10 minutes
Standing time: 5 minutes

- 2 **slices bacon**
- 2 **tablespoons finely chopped onion**
- 1 **8-ounce can tomatoes, cut up**
- ⅓ **cup water**
- ½ **teaspoon sugar**
- ½ **teaspoon instant chicken bouillon granules**
- ¼ **teaspoon dried basil, crushed**
  Dash chili powder
- ½ **cup quick-cooking rice**
- 1 **tablespoon snipped parsley**

In a medium saucepan cook bacon till crisp. Remove and drain bacon on paper toweling, reserving drippings in saucepan. Crumble bacon and set aside.

Add the chopped onion to the drippings in the saucepan; cook till the onion is tender but not brown. Stir the *undrained* tomatoes, water, sugar, chicken bouillon granules, dried basil, and chili powder into the cooked onion. Bring the tomato mixture to boiling. Stir in the quick-cooking rice. Cover the rice mixture and let stand about 5 minutes or till the liquid is absorbed.

Stir reserved bacon pieces into rice. Heat through. Before serving, sprinkle with the snipped parsley. Makes 2 servings.

Rainbow Sherbet Parfaits

Preparation time: 5 minutes

- **Lime sherbet***
- **Orange sherbet***
- **Pineapple *or* strawberry topping**
- 1 **strawberry, halved (optional)**

Alternate layers of lime and orange sherbet and pineapple or strawberry topping in 2 parfait glasses. Freeze till serving time. Before serving, garnish each parfait with a strawberry half, if desired. Makes 2 servings.
***Note:** Instead of layering two kinds of sherbet, just spoon rainbow sherbet into the two parfait glasses.

Chocolate Ribbon Parfaits

Assembling time: 10 minutes

- 2 **tablespoons dairy sour cream *or* plain yogurt**
- 1 **5-ounce can chocolate fudge pudding**
- 1 **5-ounce can strawberry, vanilla, butterscotch, *or* banana pudding**
- ¼ **cup granola**

Stir *1 tablespoon* of the dairy sour cream or yogurt into the chocolate fudge pudding. Stir the remaining sour cream or yogurt into the strawberry, vanilla, banana, or butterscotch pudding.

Alternate layers of chocolate fudge pudding and strawberry or other pudding in 2 parfait glasses, layering twice and topping each of the pudding layers with *some* of the granola. Chill till serving time. Makes 2 servings.

Steak in Lime Sauce

Cooking time: 8 minutes

- 8 **ounces beef cubed steak**
  Salt
  Pepper
- 1 **tablespoon cooking oil**
- ½ **cup sliced fresh mushrooms**
- 1 **tablespoon butter *or* margarine**
- 2 **tablespoons water**
- 1 **tablespoon lime juice**
  Lime slices (optional)

Cut the steak into 2 serving-size portions. Sprinkle each piece of meat with salt and pepper.

In a small skillet cook steaks over medium heat in hot cooking oil about 1 minute on each side or till meat is brown on both sides; cook the steaks for 1 minute more. Remove the steaks, reserving the drippings in the skillet; set steaks aside.

To the reserved drippings in skillet add the sliced mushrooms and butter or margarine; cook about 5 minutes or till the mushrooms are tender but not brown. Stir in the water and lime juice. Bring the mixture to boiling. Return the steaks to skillet; cook for 1 minute more or till the steaks are heated through. Garnish with lime slices, if desired. Makes 2 servings.
• **Steak Piccata:** Prepare Steak in Lime Sauce as directed above, *except* substitute 1 tablespoon *lemon juice* and *lemon slices* for the lime juice and lime slices. Continue as directed above.

Beat-the-Clock Menus

MENU

Pepper Burgers
in Thyme Sauce

Tomato Slices
or Celery Sticks

French Bread Parmesan

Tropical Fruit Pudding

Carbonated Beverage

Timetable

*Total preparation time:
35 minutes*

• **About 35 minutes** before serving, prepare the Tropical Fruit Pudding and chill.
• Prepare the French bread; preheat oven.
• Shape and brown the burgers.
• Heat the bread.
• Slice tomato and celery sticks.
• Make the sauce for burgers.
• Add the burgers and green pepper strips to the sauce and heat through.

Tropical Fruit Pudding

*Assembling time: 5 minutes
Chilling time: 30 minutes*

- 1 8¾-ounce can tropical fruit salad
- 1 5-ounce can vanilla pudding
   Few drops rum flavoring

Drain the tropical fruit salad, reserving 2 tablespoons juice; set aside 2 cherries from the salad for a garnish, if desired.

In a small mixing bowl stir together the vanilla pudding, rum flavoring, and the reserved fruit salad juice.

Place the fruit salad in 2 sherbet dishes or individual dessert dishes. Spoon the vanilla pudding mixture atop the fruit salad. Chill the desserts in the refrigerator for 30 minutes or till serving time.

Before serving, place *one* of the reserved cherries from the fruit salad atop each chilled dessert, if desired. Makes 2 servings.

French Bread Parmesan

*Assembling time: 5 minutes
Cooking time: 15 minutes*

- 2 to 3 tablespoons butter *or* margarine
- 4 1-inch slices French bread
- 1 tablespoon grated Parmesan cheese

If necessary, soften the butter or margarine. Cut the butter or margarine into pieces; place in a heat-proof bowl in a cool oven. Turn the oven to 350°; heat for 3 minutes. Transfer the butter or margarine to a cool bowl to prevent melting.

Spread the butter or margarine on both sides of the French bread slices. Sprinkle the bread with Parmesan cheese.

Arrange the bread slices on an ungreased baking sheet. Bake in a 375° oven about 15 minutes or till the bread is golden brown. Makes 2 servings.

Pepper Burgers in Thyme Sauce

*Assembling time: 5 minutes
Cooking time: 20 minutes*

- 1 beaten egg
- 1 tablespoon milk
- ⅓ cup soft bread crumbs
- ¼ teaspoon salt
   Dash dried thyme, crushed
- ½ pound ground beef
- ½ small onion, sliced and separated into rings
- ½ cup cold water
- 1½ teaspoons all-purpose flour
- ½ teaspoon instant beef bouillon granules
- ½ teaspoon Worcestershire sauce
- ¼ teaspoon dried thyme, crushed
- 1 small green pepper, cut into strips

Combine egg and milk; stir in the bread crumbs, salt, and the dash thyme. Add beef; mix well. Shape into two ½-inch-thick patties.

In skillet cook patties for 3 to 4 minutes on each side or almost to desired doneness. Remove, reserving the drippings; set aside. Cook onion in reserved drippings till tender. Drain off fat.

Combine water and flour; stir in bouillon granules, the Worcestershire, and the ¼ teaspoon thyme. Stir into skillet. Cook and stir till thickened and bubbly. Cook and stir for 1 minute more. Return the burgers to skillet. Add green pepper; cover and simmer for 3 to 4 minutes more or till burgers are done. Makes 2 servings.

MENU

Chicken with
Plum-Chili Sauce

Calico Coleslaw or
Purchased Coleslaw

Potato Chips

Peppermint Sundaes

Lemonade

Peppermint Sundaes

Assembling time: 10 minutes

Fudge topping
**4 scoops peppermint *or*
chocolate ice cream**
Marshmallow topping
**Pressurized dessert
topping**
**2 tablespoons chopped
pecans**
2 maraschino cherries

In a small saucepan heat the desired amount of fudge topping over low heat, stirring occasionally.

Meanwhile, place *2 scoops* of ice cream in 2 individual dessert dishes. Spoon the marshmallow topping over the ice cream; drizzle with the hot fudge topping.

Top each dessert with dessert topping, *1 tablespoon* of the pecans, and *1* maraschino cherry. Makes 2 servings.

Timetable

*Total preparation time:
40 minutes*

• **Forty minutes** before serving, prepare the chicken and broil.
• Toss together Calico Coleslaw or use purchased coleslaw and chill.
• Turn the chicken.
• Make the sauce and brush on the chicken.
• Prepare sugar-sweetened lemonade mix according to package directions; serve over ice cubes.
• Heat the fudge topping for the sundaes.
• Make Peppermint Sundaes before serving.

Calico Coleslaw

*Assembling time: 12 minutes
Chilling time: 15 minutes*

1 cup shredded cabbage
**1 medium carrot,
shredded (½ cup)**
**2 tablespoons sliced
green onion**
2 tablespoons salad oil
1 tablespoon vinegar
½ teaspoon sugar
¼ teaspoon salt
¼ teaspoon dry mustard
**⅛ teaspoon celery seed
Dash bottled hot pepper
sauce**

For coleslaw, in a medium salad bowl combine the shredded cabbage, the shredded carrot, and sliced green onion.

For dressing, in a screw-top jar combine the salad oil, vinegar, sugar, salt, dry mustard, celery seed, and the hot pepper sauce. Cover and shake to mix well.

Pour the dressing over coleslaw. Toss lightly to coat the vegetables. Cover and chill coleslaw in the freezer for up to 15 minutes or in the refrigerator till serving time.

Toss the coleslaw again before serving. Makes 2 servings.

Chicken with Plum-Chili Sauce

*Assembling time: 5 minutes
Cooking time: 30 minutes*

**4 chicken drumsticks *or*
chicken thighs *or* 2
chicken legs *or* 1
whole medium chicken
breast, halved
lengthwise**
¼ cup chili sauce
1 tablespoon lemon juice
**1 tablespoon thinly sliced
green onion**
**1 tablespoon plum,
grape, *or* desired
fruit jelly**

Rinse chicken pieces in cold water; pat dry with paper toweling. Place chicken pieces, skin side up, on rack of unheated broiler pan. Broil chicken 5 to 6 inches from heat for 25 minutes or till nearly tender, turning the pieces once. (*Or,* grill chicken,* skin side up, over *medium-hot* coals about 35 minutes or till nearly tender, turning pieces once.)

Meanwhile, for the sauce, in a small mixing bowl combine the chili sauce; lemon juice; sliced green onion; and plum, grape, or desired fruit jelly.

Brush chicken pieces with the sauce. Broil chicken 5 to 6 inches from heat for 2 to 3 minutes more. Turn; brush again with the sauce. Broil for 2 to 3 minutes more or till tender. (*Or,* grill chicken* for 10 minutes more or till tender, turning pieces once and brushing with sauce.) Makes 2 servings.
*Note: Try the grilled version of this recipe when you have time to heat the coals.

Beat-the-Clock Menus

MENU

Zucchini Frittata

Apple Drop Biscuits
Butter or Margarine
Jam or Honey

Mixed Fruit Freeze

Coffee or Tea

Mixed Fruit Freeze

Assembling time: 5 minutes

- 1 10-ounce package frozen mixed fruit (in quick-thaw pouch)
- 1 8-ounce carton orange yogurt
- 2 tablespoons milk

Combine the frozen mixed fruit, the orange yogurt, and the milk in a blender container. Cover the container and blend till the fruit mixture is smooth. Pour the blended mixture into 2 dessert glasses. Chill desserts in the freezer till serving time. Makes 2 servings.

• **Peach Freeze:** Prepare Mixed Fruit Freeze as above, *except* substitute one 10-ounce package frozen *peach slices (in quick-thaw pouch)* for the frozen mixed fruit. Chill as directed above.

• **Mixed Fruit Cream:** Prepare the Mixed Fruit Freeze as above, *except* substitute 1 cup *vanilla or peach ice cream* for the yogurt. Chill as directed above.

Timetable

Total preparation time: 30 minutes

• **Thirty minutes** before serving, prepare and bake the Apple Drop Biscuits.
• Blend together ingredients for Mixed Fruit Freeze and chill in freezer.
• Prepare and cook Zucchini Frittata.
• Make coffee or tea.
• Garnish the frittata.

Apple Drop Biscuits

Assembling time: 10 minutes
Cooking time: 10 minutes

- 1 cup packaged biscuit mix
- 2 tablespoons chopped walnuts
- 1 tablespoon sugar
- ¼ teaspoon ground cinnamon
- ⅛ teaspoon ground nutmeg
  Dash ground cloves
- ¼ cup apple cider *or* apple juice
- ¼ cup shredded, peeled apple

In a medium mixing bowl stir together the biscuit mix, walnuts, sugar, cinnamon, nutmeg, and the cloves. Make a well in the center of ingredients.

In a small mixing bowl combine the apple cider or apple juice and the shredded apple. Add the apple mixture all at once to the center of dry ingredients. Stir just till the dough clings together.

Drop the dough biscuit from a tablespoon onto a greased baking sheet. Bake in a 450° oven for 8 to 10 minutes. Serve the biscuits warm. Makes 6 biscuits.

Zucchini Frittata

Assembling time: 5 minutes
Cooking time: 10 minutes

- 1 cup chopped zucchini
- 2 tablespoons chopped onion
- 2 tablespoons olive oil *or* cooking oil
- 4 beaten eggs
- 2 tablespoons grated Parmesan cheese
  Dash pepper
  Thin tomato wedges
- 1 tablespoon snipped parsley

In a covered 8-inch skillet cook the chopped zucchini and the 2 tablespoons chopped onion in hot olive oil or cooking oil over medium heat about 5 minutes or just till the vegetables are crisp-tender.

In a small mixing bowl stir together the beaten eggs, Parmesan cheese, and the pepper; pour over the zucchini mixture in the skillet. Cook, uncovered, till the mixture begins to set around the edges. As the egg mixture begins to set, run a spatula around the edge of the skillet, lifting the mixture to allow uncooked portion to flow underneath cooked portion.

Loosen the sides and bottom of the frittata with the spatula. Serve the frittata from the skillet. (Or, if desired, gently slide the frittata, faceup, onto a serving platter). Garnish the frittata with the thin tomato wedges and the snipped parsley. Serve the frittata immediately. Makes 2 servings.

MENU

Creamed Eggs and Broccoli

Spiced Prunes

Orange Tea

Spiced Prunes

Cooking time: 10 minutes

8 **pitted, dried prunes**
¾ **cup water**
1 **tablespoon brown sugar**
1 **inch stick cinnamon** *or*
   ¼ **teaspoon ground cinnamon**
3 **whole allspice** *or* **dash ground allspice**
1 **whole clove** *or* **dash ground cloves**

In a 1-quart saucepan combine the prunes, water, brown sugar, cinnamon stick or ground cinnamon, whole allspice or ground allspice, and the whole clove or ground cloves.

Bring the mixture to boiling; reduce heat. Simmer, covered, for 10 minutes. Remove the cinnamon stick, whole allspice, and whole clove, if using the whole spices. (If using ground spices, omit this step).

Serve prunes warm or chilled. To serve chilled, cover prunes and chill in the freezer for 15 minutes. Makes 2 servings.

Timetable

Total preparation time: 35 minutes

• **Thirty-five minutes** before serving, hard-cook the eggs.
• Prepare Spiced Prunes and set aside or chill in the freezer for 15 minutes.
• Warm the teapot.
• Peel and chop the eggs.
• Heat the Canadian bacon.
• Toast the English muffins.
• Make the broccoli sauce.
• Make Orange Tea.

Creamed Eggs and Broccoli

Cooking time: 30 minutes

2 **eggs**
1 **10-ounce package frozen cut broccoli with cheese sauce**
⅓ **cup dairy sour cream**
4 **slices Canadian-style bacon**
2 **English muffins, split Butter** *or* **margarine**

To hard-cook the eggs, place in a small saucepan; cover the eggs with cold water. Bring to boiling; reduce heat to just below simmering. Cover and cook for 15 minutes. Run cold water over eggs till cool. Remove shells; chop eggs.

Cook the broccoli with cheese sauce according to package directions. Open plastic cooking bag.

Place the sour cream in a 1-quart saucepan. Gradually stir the broccoli with cheese sauce and chopped eggs into the sour cream. Heat through over low heat, stirring occasionally.

Meanwhile, in a skillet heat the Canadian bacon. Toast the English muffin halves and spread with butter or margarine. Place *one* slice of Canadian bacon on *each* English muffin half; top with the broccoli mixture. Makes 2 servings.

Orange Tea

Assembling time: 5 minutes
Standing time: 5 minutes

Boiling water
2 **teaspoons loose tea** *or* **2 tea bags**
½ **teaspoon finely shredded orange peel** *or* **one 2-inch-long orange-peel strip**
2 **cups boiling water**
1 **to 2 teaspoons honey**
2 **orange slices (optional)**

To warm the teapot, fill with the boiling water; let stand several minutes or till the teapot is warm. Measure the loose tea and finely shredded orange peel into tea ball. (*Or,* use the tea bags and the orange-peel strip.)

Empty the teapot. Add the tea ball or the tea bags and orange-peel strip to the teapot. Immediately add the 2 cups boiling water to the warm teapot. Cover the teapot and let the tea steep for 3 to 5 minutes or till of desired strength.

Remove the tea ball or the tea bags and orange-peel strip. Stir the honey into tea.

Pour the tea into 2 teacups. Garnish each serving with an orange slice, if desired. Makes 2 (8-ounce) servings.

• **Orange Iced Tea:** Prepare the Orange Tea as directed above, *except* use 3 teaspoons *loose tea or 3 tea bags.* Stir in the honey. Cool to room temperature. Cover and chill. Stir again before serving. Pour over *ice cubes* in glasses. Garnish as directed above. Makes 2 (8-ounce) servings.

Low-Cost Meals

MENU

Ham and Potato Puffs

Fruit Plate with Ginger Dressing

**Rye Muffins
Butter or Margarine**

Java Eggnog

Beverage

Even though food prices are continually soaring, you can prepare these delicious dinners for pennies a serving. And to make these meals even less expensive, we suggest using a little supermarket savvy when you are shopping for the ingredients.

When you shop for food, consider whether the lower-priced store brands or generic products will serve your needs. And weigh the economy of buying a large package size versus a small one. Generally the bigger size is the better buy, but not if you have limited storage space or if the food has a short shelf life.

Be attuned to seasonal availability of foods such as fruits and vegetables. When in season, the fresh form may cost less than the frozen and even canned forms.

Analyze the cost of all convenience food products. As a rule, the more precutting, prepackaging, and premixing involved in producing these products for the market shelf, the higher the price. Is the time they'll save you worth their extra cost?

Timetable

• **About 1½ hours** before serving, cook and mash the potato for the puffs.

• Meanwhile, make the sauce for puffs.

• Prepare the muffin batter and spoon into muffin pans.

• Finish making Ham and Potato Puffs and bake.

• Put muffins in the oven with the puffs, after the puffs have been baking about 5 minutes.

• Prepare the fruit and dressing; cover and chill.

• **Before serving,** arrange Fruit Plate with Ginger Dressing.

• Make Java Eggnog.

• Make beverage.

Rye Muffins

½   cup all-purpose flour
¼   cup rye flour
2   tablespoons brown
     sugar
1   teaspoon baking powder
¼   to ½ teaspoon caraway
     seed
¼   teaspoon salt
1   beaten egg
⅓   cup milk
2   tablespoons cooking oil

In a medium mixing bowl stir together the all-purpose flour, rye flour, brown sugar, baking powder, caraway seed, and the salt. Make a well in the center of the dry ingredients; set aside.

In another mixing bowl combine the beaten egg, milk, and cooking oil. Add the milk mixture all at once to the center of the dry ingredients. Stir just till the dry ingredients are moistened (the batter should be lumpy).

Grease a muffin pan; fill the muffin cups ½ full with batter. Bake the muffins in a 350° oven for 20 to 25 minutes or till golden. Remove muffins from pans. Serve warm. Makes 5 muffins.

Fruit Plate with Ginger Dressing

Use the pomegranate seed option in September when fresh pomegranates are not only at the peak of their growing season but also at their lowest price—

1 medium orange
3 tablespoons honey
⅛ teaspoon ground ginger
1 medium apple, cored and sliced
1 medium banana, sliced
   Lettuce leaves
2 tablespoons dried currants, raisins, chopped pitted dates, *or* pomegranate seeds

For dressing, section the orange over a mixing bowl, catching the orange juice; set orange sections aside. Add the honey and ground ginger to the orange juice; stir with a fork till ingredients are combined.

Add orange sections, *unpeeled* apple slices, and banana slices to the orange juice dressing. Toss the fruit lightly with the orange juice dressing to coat, preventing apple and banana slices from darkening. Cover and chill till serving time.

Before serving, drain the fruit mixture, reserving the dressing. Arrange the orange sections, apple slices, and the banana slices on 2 lettuce-lined individual salad plates. Pour the reserved orange juice dressing atop. Sprinkle the fruit plate with currants, raisins, chopped dates, or pomegranate seeds. Makes 2 servings.

Ham and Potato Puffs

1 medium potato, peeled and cut up
1 tablespoon butter *or* margarine
1 tablespon all-purpose flour
¼ teaspoon salt*
¼ teaspoon dried basil, crushed
   Dash pepper
⅔ cup milk
½ cup chopped cooked ham, pork, beef, lamb, chicken, *or* turkey
½ cup diced cooked vegetables *or* ½ of an 8¼-ounce can mixed vegetables, drained
1 egg yolk
⅓ cup shredded brick, Monterey Jack, Swiss, *or* cheddar cheese
1 egg white

In a medium saucepan cook the potato in boiling water till tender. Drain and mash potato; set aside (should have about ½ cup).

In a medium saucepan melt the butter or margarine; stir in the flour, salt,* basil, and pepper. Add the milk all at once; cook and stir till the mixture is thickened and bubbly. Cook and stir for 1 minute more. Remove from heat. Stir in the meat and vegetables. Turn the mixture into two 10-ounce custard cups or two 12-ounce soufflé dishes.

In a small bowl beat the egg yolk with a fork. Stir egg yolk into mashed potatoes along with the cheese. In a small mixer bowl beat the egg white on high speed of electric mixer till stiff peaks form (tips stand straight); fold into the potato mixture.

Spoon the potato mixture atop the meat mixture in dishes. Bake in a 350° oven about 25 minutes or till top is golden. Serve immediately. Makes 2 servings.

*Note: Omit salt if using ham.

Java Eggnog

Adjust the level of coffee to suit your taste—

1 egg yolk
2 tablespoons sugar
1 cup milk
1 to 2 teaspoons instant coffee crystals
¼ teaspoon vanilla
   Dash salt
½ cup whipping cream
1 egg white
1 tablespoon sugar
   Dash ground nutmeg (optional)

In a small mixer bowl beat the egg yolk on high speed of an electric mixer. Gradually add the 2 tablespoons sugar, beating on high speed about 4 minutes or till thick and lemon colored. Stir in the milk. Stir in the coffee crystals, vanilla, and salt. Cover and chill the mixture till serving time.

Before serving, in a medium mixer bowl whip the cream till soft peaks form; set aside.

Wash the beaters thoroughly. In a small mixer bowl beat the egg white till soft peaks form (tips curl over). Gradually add the 1 tablespoon sugar, beating till stiff peaks form (tips stand straight).

Fold the chilled egg yolk mixture and whipped cream into the beaten egg white. Serve immediately. To serve, pour the eggnog into mugs or cups. Sprinkle each serving with ground nutmeg, if desired. Makes 2 (8-ounce) servings.

Low-Cost Meals

Timetable

- **About one hour** before serving, start coals if grilling chicken.
- Prepare and bake Rosy Apple Cobbler.
- Prepare the chicken and the herb mixture.
- Grill or broil the chicken.
- Cook frozen potato nuggets according to package directions.
- Turn and brush the chicken.
- Cook Green Beans Piquant.
- Make coffee or tea.

Rosy Apple Cobbler

2 medium apples, peeled, cored, and sliced (2 cups)
⅔ cup cranberry juice cocktail
3 tablespoons sugar
1 tablespoon all-purpose flour
⅛ teaspoon ground nutmeg
⅓ cup packaged biscuit mix
2 teaspoons sugar
¼ teaspoon finely shredded lemon peel
4 teaspoons milk

For filling, in a medium saucepan combine the apple slices and cranberry juice cocktail. Cover and cook for 5 to 8 minutes, stirring occasionally.

In a mixing bowl combine the 3 tablespoons sugar, the flour, and nutmeg; add to the apple mixture. Cook and stir till thickened and bubbly. Cook and stir for 1 minute more; keep warm.

Meanwhile, for biscuit topper, in a small mixing bowl stir together the biscuit mix, the 2 teaspoons sugar, and lemon peel. Stir in the milk.

Turn the hot apple filling into a 20-ounce casserole. Immediately spoon the biscuit topper in 2 mounds atop. Bake in a 400° oven about 20 minutes or till biscuit topper is done. Makes 2 servings.

Green Beans Piquant

1 8-ounce can cut green beans *or* 1 cup frozen cut green beans
1 small onion, thinly sliced
1 tablespoon cooked bacon pieces
1 tablespoon vinegar
1 teaspoon sugar
½ teaspoon Worcestershire sauce

In a medium saucepan combine *undrained* canned green beans and sliced onion. Cover and cook about 7 minutes or till the onion is tender. (Or, cook frozen green beans according to the package directions, adding onion.) Drain the bean mixture.

Stir the cooked bacon pieces, vinegar, sugar, and the Worcestershire sauce into the drained bean mixture. Cover and heat through. Makes 2 servings.

Herb-Basted Chicken

4 chicken drumsticks *or* chicken thighs *or* 2 chicken legs *or* 1 whole medium chicken breast, halved lengthwise
1 tablespoon finely chopped onion
1 tablespoon cooking oil
2 teaspoons finely snipped parsley
2 teaspoons vinegar
1 teaspoon honey
1 teaspoon snipped fresh thyme *or* ¼ teaspoon dried thyme, crushed
½ teaspoon snipped fresh rosemary *or* ⅛ teaspoon dried rosemary, crushed
⅛ teaspoon salt
Sprigs fresh thyme *or* rosemary (optional)

Rinse the chicken pieces in cold water; pat dry with paper toweling. In a small mixing bowl combine the finely chopped onion, cooking oil, snipped parsley, the vinegar, honey, fresh or dried thyme, fresh or dried rosemary, and salt. Brush chicken pieces lightly with the herb mixture.

Place the chicken, skin side down, over *medium-hot* coals. Grill for 20 minutes or till skin side is brown. Turn and grill for 15 to 20 minutes more or till chicken is tender, brushing with herb mixture occasionally. (Or, broil chicken, skin side down, 5 to 6 inches from heat for 15 minutes; turn and broil about 15 minutes more or till tender. Brush with herb mixture often during last 3 minutes of broiling.) Garnish chicken with sprigs of thyme or rosemary, if desired. Makes 2 servings.

MENU

Parmesan Fried Fish

Cream of Fresh Tomato Soup

Vegetable Pilaf

Fresh Fruit

Beverage

Timetable

• **Several hours** before serving, thaw the pan-dressed fish or fish fillets, if frozen.
• **About 35 minutes** before serving, cook Vegetable Pilaf.
• Make Cream of Fresh Tomato Soup.
• Prepare the coating for fish.
• Coat and fry the fish.
• Make the beverage and prepare fresh fruit, if necessary.

Cream of Fresh Tomato Soup

 2 medium tomatoes, chopped (2 cups)
 2 tablespoons chopped onion
 1 small bay leaf
 ¼ teaspoon sugar
 ¼ teaspoon salt
   Dash pepper
 1 tablespoon butter *or* margarine
 1 tablespoon all-purpose flour
 ⅛ teaspoon salt
 1 cup milk
   Snipped parsley *or* snipped chives

In a saucepan combine the tomatoes, onion, bay leaf, sugar, the ¼ teaspoon salt, and the pepper. Bring the mixture to boiling; reduce heat. Cover and simmer for 10 minutes. Strain the hot tomato mixture and set aside (should have about 1 cup).

In the same saucepan melt the butter or margarine; stir in the flour and the ⅛ teaspoon salt. Add the milk all at once; cook and stir till the mixture is thickened and bubbly. Cook and stir for 1 minute more. Gradually stir the strained tomato mixture into the thickened mixture in saucepan.

To serve, ladle the soup into two bowls. Garnish each serving with snipped parsley or chives. Makes 2 servings.

Vegetable Pilaf

 ¼ cup long grain rice
 1 tablespoon finely chopped onion
 1 tablespoon butter *or* margarine
 ¾ cup frozen mixed vegetables
 ⅔ cup water
 1 teaspoon instant chicken bouillon granules

In a small saucepan cook the uncooked rice and finely chopped onion in hot butter or margarine, stirring frequently, for 5 to 10 minutes or till the rice is light brown and the onion pieces are tender but not brown.

Stir the mixed vegetables, water, and instant chicken bouillon granules into the rice mixture in the saucepan. Bring the mixture to boiling; reduce heat. Cover and cook the mixture about 20 minutes or till the liquid is absorbed and the rice and mixed vegetables are tender. Makes 2 servings.

Parmesan Fried Fish

 8 ounces fresh *or* frozen pan-dressed fish *or* fish fillets
 2 tablespoons all-purpose flour
   Dash garlic salt
 1 beaten egg
 2 tablespoons milk
 ¼ cup finely crushed saltine crackers
 2 tablespoons grated Parmesan cheese
 1 tablespoon finely snipped parsley
 ½ cup cooking oil *or* shortening
   Lemon slices (optional)
   Parsley sprig (optional)

Thaw fish, if frozen. Rinse and pat dry with paper toweling. In a shallow dish combine the flour and garlic salt; set aside. In another shallow dish combine the beaten egg and milk; set aside. Combine the crushed crackers, Parmesan cheese, and the 1 tablespoon snipped parsley.

Coat the fish with flour mixture. Dip fish in egg mixture, coating both sides. Then roll the fish in crumb mixture to coat evenly.

In a skillet heat cooking oil or shortening; add the fish in a single layer to skillet. If fillets have skin on, fry skin side last. Fry fish over medium heat on one side for 4 to 5 minutes. Turn and fry for 4 to 5 minutes more. The fish is done when both sides are brown and crisp and when fish flakes easily when tested with a fork. Drain on paper toweling. Garnish the fish with lemon slices and a parsley sprig, if desired. Makes 2 servings.

Make-Ahead Menus

MENU

Herbed Lamb Kabobs

Tabouleh Salad

Cucumber Slices

Pita Bread

Frozen Orange Tarts or Frozen Orange Cups

Sugar Cookies

Coffee

No matter how much you may enjoy cooking, you don't have to be tied to your apron strings right before every meal. By planning and preparing the major part of your meal ahead, the two of you can treat yourselves to some last-minute free time.

These three meals will give you a head start on your food preparation well before the meal. To guide you, we've provided both the advance and the final preparation timings for each of the following menus. Individual timings are given with each recipe, too.

Whenever you're cooking food ahead of time, be sure to store foods properly. Whether a food is to be refrigerated or frozen, you should wrap or seal it tightly in moisture-vaporproof wrap or in freezer containers. Label each package with the contents, final preparation instructions, number of servings, and the date.

In make-ahead cookery, there are a few general guidelines to follow. You should freeze most casseroles before rather than after baking. Exceptions include dishes containing uncooked rice, raw vegetables, and uncooked meat or frozen meat that has been thawed.

To prevent any cooked vegetables from overcooking during reheating, undercook them slightly before storage.

Try to use cooking oil, shortening, butter, and margarine sparingly because these fats do not blend well when reheated.

Since flavoring agents such as garlic, onion, and peppers intensify over a period of time, season foods lightly before storing.

Toppings like chopped nuts, crumbs, and cheese should be added during final preparation.

Even if you aren't assembling a whole meal in advance, you can still apply make-ahead cooking principles. For example, you can prepare and store ingredients in quantity. Chopped onions, shredded or grated cheese, and toasted coconut and nuts are all great made-ahead time-savers to have on hand.

You'll find that once you have prepared most or all of your meal ahead of time, you can relax as the dining hour draws near.

Timetable

Total advance preparation time: 1 hour and 15 minutes
Total final preparation time: 20 minutes

- **Several hours** or the day before serving, soak the bulgur.
- Cook the onion wedges.
- Prepare marinade and marinate lamb; cover and chill.
- Make Frozen Orange Tarts or Frozen Orange Cups and freeze.
- Prepare Tabouleh Salad; cover and chill till serving time.
- **About 1 hour** before serving, heat the coals to grill lamb.
- **Twenty minutes** before serving, finish preparing the Herbed Lamb Kabobs and grill.
- Arrange the Tabouleh Salad.
- Make coffee.
- Take dessert out of freezer.

Tabouleh Salad

Advance preparation time:
1¼ hours
Final preparation time:
5 minutes

- ½ **cup boiling water**
- ¼ **cup bulgur wheat**
- ¼ **cup snipped parsley**
- ¼ **cup finely chopped cucumber**
- 1 **tablespoon finely chopped green onion**
- 1 **tablespoon snipped fresh mint *or* 1 teaspoon dried mint leaves, crushed**
- 1 **tablespoon olive oil *or* cooking oil**
- ¼ **teaspoon salt**
  Dash pepper
- 2 **pita bread rounds, cut in half crosswise, *or* shredded lettuce**
- ¼ **cup plain yogurt (optional)**
- 1 **small tomato, chopped (optional)**

For tabouleh, pour boiling water over bulgur wheat; let stand for 1 hour. Drain well, squeezing out excess water. Combine the drained bulgur wheat, snipped parsley, chopped cucumber, green onion, fresh or dried mint, olive or cooking oil, salt, and pepper. Cover and chill at least 1 hour.

Before serving, place the pita bread or shredded lettuce on 2 serving plates. Spoon tabouleh mixture into pita bread pockets or atop lettuce. Garnish with yogurt and chopped tomato, if desired. Makes 2 servings.

Frozen Orange Tarts

Advance preparation time:
30 minutes
Final preparation time:
15 minutes

- 1 **cup crushed vanilla wafers**
- 2 **tablespoons finely chopped walnuts**
- 3 **tablespoons butter *or* margarine, melted**
- ¼ **cup sugar**
- 2 **tablespoons frozen orange juice concentrate, thawed**
- 1 **egg white**
- ½ **cup dairy sour cream**
  Pressurized dessert topping (optional)

For tart shells, combine crushed wafers and walnuts. Stir in the melted butter or margarine. Place 6 paper bake cups in a muffin pan. Press the crumb mixture into the cups, covering sides and bottom.

In a mixer bowl combine the sugar, orange juice concentrate, and the egg white. Beat at medium speed of electric mixer about 10 minutes or till soft peaks form (tips curl over). Gently fold in the sour cream. Spoon the orange juice mixture into prepared tart shells. Freeze till firm.

Before serving, let tarts stand at room temperature for 10 to 15 minutes. Garnish with the dessert topping, if desired. Makes 6 tarts.
•**Frozen Orange Cups:** Prepare Frozen Orange Tarts as above, *except* omit pressing crumb mixture into paper bake cups.

For orange cups, slice off top quarters of 2 medium *oranges.* Scoop out orange pulp (reserve pulp for later use). Scallop edges of orange cups, if desired.

Spoon the crumb mixture into orange cups, reserving 2 tablespoons crumbs. Spoon the orange mixture atop crumb layer. Sprinkle with reserved crumbs. Continue as directed above.

Herbed Lamb Kabobs

Advance preparation time:
25 minutes
Final preparation time:
20 minutes

- ½ **medium onion, cut into wedges**
- ¼ **cup cooking oil**
- ¼ **cup lemon juice**
- 2 **tablespoons chopped onion**
- 2 **tablespoons snipped parsley**
- 1 **small clove garlic, minced**
- ¼ **teaspoon salt**
- ¼ **teaspoon dried marjoram, crushed**
- ¼ **teaspoon dried thyme, crushed**
- ⅛ **teaspoon pepper**
- ½ **pound boneless lamb, cut into 1-inch pieces**
- ½ **medium sweet green *or* red pepper, cut into squares**

In a saucepan cook the onion wedges in boiling water about 25 minutes or till tender; drain.

Meanwhile, for marinade, in a mixing bowl combine cooking oil, lemon juice, the 2 tablespoons chopped onion, the snipped parsley, garlic, salt, marjoram, thyme, and the pepper.

Stir the lamb pieces into the marinade. Cover and chill the onion wedges and the lamb in the refrigerator for 6 to 8 hours or overnight, stirring occasionally.

Before serving, drain the lamb, reserving the marinade. Thread 4 small skewers with lamb pieces, onion wedges, and sweet green or red pepper squares. Grill the kabobs over *hot* coals for 10 to 12 minutes or to desired doneness, turning the kabobs several times and brushing often with reserved marinade. Makes 2 servings.

Make-Ahead Menus

MENU

Beef-Zucchini Bake

Marinated Lima Beans

Breadsticks

Rhubarb Ice Cream

Iced Tea

Marinated Lima Beans

Advance preparation time:
5 minutes
Final preparation time:
5 minutes

2 tablespoons vinegar
1 tablespoon salad oil
2 teaspoons prepared horseradish
1 teaspoon sugar
1 8½-ounce can lima beans, drained
2 tablespoons chopped green pepper
1 tablespoon chopped onion
1 tablespoon chopped pimiento
Lettuce cups (optional)

For marinade, in a medium mixing bowl combine the vinegar, salad oil, prepared horseradish, and the sugar.

Stir the drained lima beans, chopped green pepper, chopped onion, and chopped pimiento into the marinade. Cover and chill the lima bean mixture in marinade in refrigerator for at least 3 hours or overnight.

To serve, with a slotted spoon, spoon the bean mixture into lettuce cups, if desired. Makes 2 servings.

Timetable

Total advance preparation time:
45 minutes
Final preparation time:
65 minutes

• **Several hours** or a few days before serving, make Rhubarb Ice Cream; cover and freeze.
• Marinate the lima beans; cover and chill.
• Cook the macaroni and the beef mixture. Assemble the casserole; cover and freeze.
• Make iced tea and chill.
• **Sixty-five minutes** before serving, bake the Beef-Zucchini Bake.

Rhubarb Ice Cream

Advance preparation time:
20 minutes

1 cup diced fresh *or* frozen rhubarb
¼ cup sugar
2 tablespoons water
1 to 2 drops red food coloring (optional)
1 cup frozen whipped dessert topping, thawed

In a saucepan combine the fresh or frozen rhubarb, sugar, and water. Bring to boiling; reduce heat. Cover and simmer for 10 minutes or till the rhubarb is tender. Remove from heat. Stir in red food coloring, if desired. Cover and chill in the freezer for 10 minutes.

Fold the dessert topping into chilled rhubarb mixture. Spoon the rhubarb mixture into two 10-ounce custard cups. Cover and freeze overnight or till the ice cream is firm. Makes 2 servings.

Beef-Zucchini Bake

Advance preparation time:
20 minutes
Final preparation time:
65 minutes

¼ cup elbow macaroni
½ pound ground beef
⅓ cup chopped onion
1 8-ounce can tomato sauce
1 medium zucchini, thinly sliced (1 cup)
¼ teaspoon salt
⅛ teaspoon fennel seed, crushed
⅛ teaspoon pepper
3 tablespoons shredded mozzarella cheese

In a saucepan cook the elbow macaroni according to package directions. Drain and set the macaroni aside.

In an 8-inch skillet cook the ground beef and onion till the beef is brown and the onion is tender; drain off fat.

Stir the cooked macaroni, the tomato sauce, sliced zucchini, salt, fennel seed, and pepper into the cooked beef mixture. Turn the mixture into a 1-quart casserole. Cover the mixture in casserole with moisture-vaporproof wrap. Seal, label, and freeze.

Before serving, remove wrap and bake frozen beef casserole, covered, in a 400° oven about 1 hour or till heated through. Sprinkle with the mozzarella cheese and bake, uncovered, about 5 minutes more or till the cheese is melted. Makes 2 servings.

MENU

Oriental Pork Chops

Hot Cooked Rice

Pea Pod Salad

Nectarines Royale

Herbal Tea

Pea Pod Salad

Advance preparation time:
10 minutes
Final preparation time:
5 minutes

    1 cup fresh pea pods *or*
        sugar snap peas *or* ½
        of a 6-ounce package
        frozen pea pods,
        thawed
    ¼ cup salad oil
    3 tablespoons white wine
        vinegar
    ¼ teaspoon salt
    ¼ teaspoon sugar
    ¼ teaspoon dried basil,
        crushed
    ⅓ cup sliced fresh
        mushrooms
        Fresh watercress *or* torn
        fresh spinach
        Alfalfa sprouts

If desired, cook pea pods or snap peas in boiling salted water for 1 to 2 minutes or till crisp-tender; drain. Cover and chill pea pods.

For dressing, in a screw-top jar combine salad oil, wine vinegar, salt, sugar, and basil. Cover the jar tightly and shake well to mix.

Pour dressing over the sliced mushrooms; toss lightly to coat. Cover and chill at least 3 hours or overnight.

Before serving, add the pea pods to mushroom mixture; toss lightly to coat.

Arrange the watercress or the torn spinach on 2 individual salad plates. With a slotted spoon, spoon vegetables atop. Garnish with the sprouts. Makes 2 servings.

Timetable

Total advance preparation time:
40 minutes
Total final preparation time:
50 minutes

• **Several hours** or the day before serving, prepare marinade and marinate pork chops; chill.
• Prepare salad; cover and chill.
• Prepare nectarines and chill.
• **Fifty minutes** before serving, grill the pork chops.
• Cook rice.
• Arrange Pea Pod Salad.
• Brew tea.
• Assemble Nectarines Royale.

Nectarines Royale

Advance preparation time:
10 minutes
Final preparation time:
5 minutes

    2 medium nectarines
    ⅓ cup sugar
    ⅓ cup water
    1 tablespoon brandy
    ½ teaspoon vanilla
    3 tablespoons dairy sour
        cream
    2 teaspoons powdered
        sugar
    1 teaspoon brandy

Plunge the nectarines into boiling water for 30 seconds to loosen skins. Peel nectarines; remove the pits and cut into quarters.

In a small saucepan combine the nectarine quarters, sugar, and water. Bring to boiling; simmer for 1 minute. Remove from heat. Stir in the 1 tablespoon brandy and the vanilla. Chill for at least 4 hours or till serving time.

Before serving, spoon the fruit into 2 individual dessert dishes. In a mixing bowl combine the sour cream, the powdered sugar, and the 1 teaspoon brandy; spoon over fruit. Makes 2 servings.

Oriental Pork Chops

Advance preparation time:
15 minutes
Final preparation time:
55 minutes

    3 tablespoons soy sauce
    2 tablespoons cooking oil
    2 tablespoons finely
        chopped green pepper
    1 teaspoon finely
        shredded orange peel
    2 tablespoons orange
        juice
    1 teaspoon brown sugar
    ½ teaspoon ground ginger
    2 pork loin rib chops,
        cut 1¼ to 1½ inches
        thick

For marinade, in a mixing bowl combine soy sauce, cooking oil, green pepper, orange peel, orange juice, brown sugar, and the ground ginger.

Place the pork chops in a plastic bag set in a bowl. Pour the marinade over meat; close the bag. Marinate the meat in the refrigerator at least 3 hours or overnight, turning bag occasionally to distribute the marinade.

Before serving, drain the pork chops, reserving marinade. Grill chops over *medium-slow* coals for 25 minutes. Brush the chops with *some* of the reserved marinade. Turn chops and grill, covered, 25 to 30 minutes more. (*Or*, broil chops 3 to 4 inches from heat for 30 minutes, turning once during cooking.) Brush the chops with the reserved marinade occasionally. Makes 2 servings.

Calorie-Trimmed Meals

Loosing weight ceases to be a lonely task when you share these light, satisfying meals with somebody else. The following menus allow you to eat a variety of food while cutting back on calories .

To help you determine where your food energy originates, we have included a calorie count for each recipe along with the total tally for each menu.*

For consistant results, we have made several assumptions—
• When two ingredient options appear in a recipe, the calorie count is based on the first ingredient option only.
• For meat recipes, the computations have been calculated using measurements for cooked lean meat, trimmed of fat.
• Any suggested garnishes and optional ingredients have been excluded from the calorie counts.
*Note: These figures were computed from the *Agriculture Handbook Number 456,* published by the United States Department of Agriculture.

Timetable

• **At least 3 hours** before serving, prepare Sun Tea or Iced Tea.
• **About 1 hour** before serving, take the fish out of freezer to partially thaw.
• Prepare and bake the Peach Custard Tarts in a 350° oven; remove tarts. Increase the oven temperature to 450°.
• Meanwhile, begin cooking the wild rice for Wild Rice with Mushrooms.
• Prepare and bake Vegetable-Topped Fish.
• Cook the brussels sprouts.
• Finish preparing Wild Rice with Mushrooms.
• Prepare the orange sauce.

Wild Rice with Mushrooms

110 calories per serving

⅓ **cup wild rice**
1 **cup water**
¼ **teaspoon salt**
½ **cup chopped fresh mushrooms**
1 **teaspoon butter *or* margarine**
Dash ground nutmeg

Run cold water over uncooked rice in a strainer for 1 minute, lifting the rice to rinse well.

In a saucepan combine rice, the 1 cup water, and salt. Bring to boiling; reduce heat. Cover and simmer for 40 minutes.

Add the chopped mushrooms to wild rice. Cover and cook for 5 to 10 minutes more or till the rice is tender and most of the liquid is absorbed. Drain well. Stir in the butter or margarine and nutmeg. Makes 2 servings.

Vegetable-Topped Fish

261 calories per serving

   8 ounces frozen fish fillets
 ½ of a small onion, sliced
      and separated into
      rings
   2 tablespoons chopped
      celery
   1 small tomato, peeled,
      seeded, and chopped
 ½ of a small green pepper,
      cut into strips
   2 teaspoons snipped
      parsley
1½ teaspoons lemon juice
 ¼ teaspoon dried dillweed
      Salt
      Pepper

Unwrap frozen fish; let stand at room temperature for 20 minutes. Meanwhile, in a small saucepan cook onion and celery in a small amount of boiling water till tender; drain. Stir the chopped tomato, the green pepper strips, snipped parsley, the lemon juice, and the dillweed into celery and onion.

With a sharp knife, cut the partially thawed fish into 2x2-inch blocks. Arrange the blocks of fish in an ungreased 8x6½x2-inch baking dish; sprinkle with the salt and pepper. Spoon the vegetable mixture over fish blocks. Bake, covered, in a 450° oven for 18 to 20 minutes or till fish flakes easily when tested with a fork. To serve, with a slotted spatula lift fish and vegetables to 2 dinner plates.* Makes 2 servings.
*Note: For a different serving presentation, spoon *some* of the orange sauce from the Brussels Sprouts in Orange Sauce onto the plates. Arrange fish and vegetables atop.

Brussels Sprouts in Orange Sauce

46 calories per serving

   1 cup fresh *or* frozen
      brussels sprouts,
      halved
 ¼ cup orange juice
 ½ teaspoon cornstarch
 ⅛ teaspoon salt
      Dash pepper

In a medium saucepan cook the fresh brussels sprouts in a small amount of boiling salted water for 15 minutes or till tender. (*Or*, cook frozen brussels sprouts according to package directions.) Drain the brussels sprout halves and set aside.

Meanwhile, in a small saucepan combine the orange juice, cornstarch, the salt, and pepper. Cook and stir till mixture is thickened and bubbly. Cook and stir for 2 minutes more.* Stir in the cooked brussels sprout halves and heat through. Makes 2 servings.
*Note: If desired, serve the orange sauce with the Vegetable-Topped Fish for this menu.

Sun Tea

0 calories per serving

   2 tea bags
   3 cups cold water
      Ice cubes
   2 lemon slices (optional)

In a 1-quart clear glass container place tea bags. Add cold water and cover. Let stand in full sun* for 2 to 3 hours or till of desired strength. Remove the tea bags. Serve over ice cubes in 2 tall glasses. If desired, serve the tea with a lemon slice. Makes 2 (12-ounce) servings.
*Note: You don't need the sun to brew Sun Tea. Prepare as directed above, *except* let tea stand at room temperature for several hours or till of desired strength.

Peach Custard Tarts

123 calories per serving

   1 8-ounce can peach slices
      (juice pack)
      or one 8-ounce can
      low-calorie unpeeled
      apricot halves,
      drained and chopped
   1 beaten egg
 ½ cup skim milk
   1 tablespoon sugar
 ¼ teaspoon vanilla
      Few drops rum flavoring
      or almond extract
      Dash salt
      Dash ground cardamom
      or ground nutmeg

Place chopped peaches or apricots on paper toweling to drain thoroughly.

In a small mixing bowl combine the beaten egg, the milk, sugar, vanilla, rum flavoring or almond extract, and salt.

Place two 4½-inch tart pans or two 10-ounce custard cups in a shallow baking pan on an oven rack. If desired, reserve a few peach or apricot pieces for a garnish. Place the remaining pieces in custard cups or tart pans. Pour the egg mixture atop fruit; sprinkle with cardamom or nutmeg.

Pour boiling water into the baking pan around custard cups or tart pans to a depth of ½ inch. Bake in a 350° oven about 20 minutes or till a knife inserted near the centers comes out clean. Remove the custard cups or tart pans from the water. If desired, garnish with the reserved peach or apricot pieces. Serve warm or chilled.* Makes 2 servings.
*Note: Unmold chilled custards, if desired. First loosen edges with a spatula or knife; slip point of knife down sides to let air in. Invert the custards onto 2 dessert plates.

Calorie-Trimmed Meals

MENU

Total calories: 485

Cheesy Beef Burros
___
Radish and Pea Salad
___
Strawberry-Banana Freeze
___
Carbonated Water with a Lime Twist

Strawberry-Banana Freeze

145 calories per serving

½ **cup frozen whole unsweetened strawberries**
1 **small banana, peeled**
Lemon juice (optional)
¼ **cup evaporated skimmed milk**
1 **teaspoon sugar**
½ **teaspoon vanilla**

If desired, for garnish, cut 1 frozen strawberry in half and 2 thin slices off the banana. Brush the banana slices with lemon juice; set aside.

Wrap remaining part of banana in moisture-vaporproof wrap and freeze till firm.

Cut frozen banana into chunks. In a blender container or food processor bowl combine the banana chunks, the evaporated skimmed milk, sugar, and vanilla. Cover and blend or process till smooth. With blender or food processor running slowly, add the frozen berries, one or two at a time, through opening in lid. Blend or process the mixture till smooth. Serve immediately. Garnish each serving with a strawberry half and banana slice, if desired. Makes 2 servings.

Timetable

● **Several hours** before serving, freeze the banana for Strawberry-Banana Freeze.
● Prepare ingredients for salad.
● **About thirty minutes** before serving, cook the tomato sauce and beef for burros.
● Assemble Cheesy Beef Burros and bake.
● Arrange Radish and Pea Salad.
● Make beverage.
● **Before serving,** prepare the Strawberry-Banana Freeze.

Radish and Pea Salad

99 calories per serving

1 **cup frozen peas *or* one 8½-ounce can peas, drained**
2 **tablespoons thinly sliced radishes**
¼ **cup low-calorie Italian salad dressing**
2 **lettuce cups**

If using frozen peas, cook according to package directions; drain. If using canned peas, omit this step.

In a small mixing bowl combine the drained peas and the sliced radishes. Pour the low-calorie Italian salad dressing over; toss the mixture lightly to coat vegetables. Cover and chill for at least 3 hours or overnight.

To serve, with a slotted spoon, spoon the chilled pea salad mixture into the 2 lettuce cups. Makes 2 servings.

Cheesy Beef Burros

241 calories per serving

1 **7½-ounce can tomatoes**
2 **canned green chili peppers, rinsed and seeded**
½ **teaspoon cornstarch**
½ **teaspoon sugar**
¼ **teaspoon salt**
¼ **teaspoon ground coriander**
¼ **pound lean ground beef**
½ **cup cream-style cottage cheese with chives**
⅛ **teaspoon salt**
2 **7- *or* 8-inch flour tortillas**

In a blender container or food processor bowl combine *undrained* tomatoes, the green chili peppers, cornstarch, sugar, the ¼ teaspoon salt, and the coriander. Cover and blend or process till smooth.

For tomato sauce, turn tomato mixture into a small saucepan; cook and stir till thickened and bubbly. Cook and stir for 2 minutes more.

In a skillet cook the ground beef till brown; drain off fat. In a mixing bowl combine the beef, cottage cheese, and the ⅛ teaspoon salt.

To assemble, spread about *1 tablespoon* of the tomato sauce onto *each* tortilla. Spread *half* of the beef mixture atop the tomato sauce on *each* tortilla; roll up the tortillas jelly-roll style.

Spread *half* of the remaining tomato sauce on the bottom of an 8x6½x2-inch baking dish. Place filled tortillas, seam side down, atop the tomato sauce in the baking dish. Top with the remaining tomato sauce. Bake, uncovered, in a 375° oven for 15 to 18 minutes or till hot. Makes 2 servings.

MENU

Total calories: 480

Chicken-Filled Melon Cups

———

Zwieback

———

Peanut Butter and Date Fluff

———

Sparkling Grape Spritzer

Chicken-Filled Melon Cups

261 calories per serving

- 1 **medium cantaloupe** *or* **honeydew melon**
- ½ **cup plain yogurt**
- 2 **tablespoons orange juice**
- 1 **teaspoon honey**
- ¼ **teaspoon celery seed**
- ¾ **cup chopped cooked chicken**
- 1 **medium apple, cored and diced**
- ½ **cup sliced celery**
  Spinach leaves

Cut the cantaloupe or honeydew melon in half lengthwise. Remove seeds. Scoop out melon balls; set aside. Scrape any remaining fruit from the shells (chill remaining fruit for another use). If desired, cut the edge of each shell in a sawtooth fashion. Invert the shells onto a paper-towel-lined tray to drain. Chill.

For dressing, in a small mixing bowl stir together the yogurt, the orange juice, honey, and celery seed. Cover and chill.

In a large mixing bowl combine the melon balls, chicken, apple, and celery; spoon into the melon shells. Place the filled melon shells on 2 spinach-lined plates. Pour dressing atop. Serve immediately. Makes 2 servings.

Timetable

- **At least 3 hours** before serving, prepare Peanut Butter and Date Fluff; cover and chill.
- Scoop out the melon for Chicken-Filled Melon Cups and make the dressing; cover and chill.
- **About 20 minutes** before serving, assemble the Chicken-Filled Melon Cups.
- **Before serving,** prepare Sparkling Grape Spritzer.

Sparkling Grape Spritzer

39 calories per serving

- 1 **5½-ounce can unsweetened grape juice**
- ½ **cup lemon-lime carbonated beverage**
  Ice cubes
- 2 **lemon slices (optional)**

In a pitcher combine the unsweetened grape juice and carbonated lemon-lime beverage. Pour grape mixture over ice cubes in 2 tall glasses. Garnish each serving with a lemon slice, if desired. Makes 2 (4-ounce) servings.

Peanut Butter and Date Fluff

150 calories per serving

- 1 **teaspoon sugar**
- 1 **teaspoon unflavored gelatin**
- ½ **cup skim milk**
- 1 **egg yolk**
- 2 **pitted whole dates, snipped (1 tablespoon)**
- 1 **teaspoon creamy peanut butter**
- ¼ **teaspoon vanilla**
- 1 **egg white**
- 1 **pitted whole date, snipped (optional)**

In a small saucepan combine the sugar and gelatin. Stir in the skim milk. Cook and stir over medium heat just till the mixture thickens slightly. Slowly stir *half* of the hot mixture into the beaten egg yolk; return all of the mixture to saucepan. Cook and stir over medium heat for 1 to 2 minutes or till slightly thickened. Remove from heat. Stir in the 2 dates, peanut butter, and vanilla. Chill till the gelatin mixture is the consistency of unbeaten egg whites (partially set).

In a small mixer bowl beat the egg white on high speed of electric mixer till stiff peaks form (tips stand straight). Gently fold the beaten egg white into the chilled gelatin mixture.

Spoon the mixture into 2 individual dessert glasses or two 6-ounce custard cups. Chill for 3 hours or till firm. Garnish each serving with *half* of the 1 snipped date, if desired. Makes 2 servings.

A LA CARTE

This chapter allows you to create your own meals and snacks by choosing from a variety of dishes. You'll find everything from delicious desserts to sumptuous stews and sandwiches, including those pictured here (Sour Cream-Apple Puff, see the recipe on page 81; Bavarian Bratwurst Stew, see recipe on page 61; and Salami 'n' Cheese Vegetablewiches, see recipe on page 64). For more versatility, we have provided microwave and crockery cooker directions when appropriate.

At the end of the chapter we've included some general information on cooking for two people. There is a guide to kitchen equipment and appliances designed for cooking in small quantities. And to help you plan how much food to cook, we've drawn up a chart of serving portions for two.

We know that leftover foods and ingredients are often a problem when you're cooking for two people. So we've provided a storage chart with the timings for refrigerating and freezing most foods.

Everything that you need to make your meal planning easier is here for you.

Entrées–Meat

Steak with Sauce Provençale

2 beef top loin steaks, cut 1 inch thick (about 12 ounces)
Salt
Pepper
1 tablespoon sliced green onion
1 small clove garlic, minced
2 tablespoons butter *or* margarine
2 tablespoons dry sherry
1 medium tomato, peeled, seeded, and cut up
2 teaspoons snipped parsley
Salt
Pepper

Slash the fat edges of steaks at 1-inch intervals, being careful not to cut into the meat. Grill the steaks over *medium-hot* coals to desired doneness, allowing 6 to 9 minutes on each side for rare, 8 to 10 minutes on each side for medium, and 10 to 13 minutes on each side for well done. Season with salt and pepper.

Meanwhile, for sauce, in a small skillet cook the green onion and garlic in hot butter or margarine till tender but not brown. Add the sherry; cook and stir the mixture about 1 minute or till liquid is slightly reduced. Add tomato and parsley; heat through. (Do not allow the pieces to lose shape.) Season to taste with salt and pepper. Serve the sauce over the steaks. Makes 2 servings.

Beef Stroganoff

½ pound boneless beef sirloin steak
2 tablespoons butter *or* margarine
½ cup sliced fresh mushrooms
¼ cup chopped onion
1 small clove garlic, minced
1 tablespoon all-purpose flour
1 tablespoon catsup
½ teaspoon instant beef bouillon granules
⅛ teaspoon dry mustard
⅓ cup dairy sour cream
2 tablespoons dry white wine
Hot cooked noodles

Partially freeze beef; thinly slice meat across the grain into bite-size strips. In a skillet brown the meat in *1 tablespoon* of the hot butter or margarine. Remove meat. Add the remaining butter, the mushrooms, onion, and garlic to skillet; cook till onion is crisp-tender. Stir in the flour, catsup, bouillon granules, mustard, ¼ teaspoon *salt,* and a dash *pepper.* Add ¾ cup *water.* Cook and stir till thickened and bubbly. Cook and stir 1 minute more. Stir in the beef strips.

Stir *some* of the meat mixture into sour cream. Return all to skillet. Stir in the wine. Heat through but *do not boil.* Serve over noodles. Sprinkle with parsley, if desired. Makes 2 servings.

• **Microwave directions:** In 1½-quart nonmetal casserole combine the mushrooms, onion, garlic, and butter or margarine. Cover with glass lid or waxed paper; cook in a counter-top microwave oven on high power for 2 minutes. Stir in beef strips, wine, flour, catsup, bouillon granules, mustard, 2 tablespoons *water,* ¼ teaspoon *salt,* and dash *pepper.* Cover and micro-cook for 4 minutes, stirring twice. Stir *some* of the hot mixture into the sour cream. Return all to casserole and micro-cook for 30 seconds or till heated through.

Sauerbraten-Style Beef and Cabbage

½ pound beef stew meat, cut into 1-inch pieces
1 tablespoon cooking oil
1 cup water
2 tablespoons vinegar
1 single-serving envelope instant onion soup mix
1 bay leaf
⅓ small head cabbage, cut into 2 wedges
1 medium potato, peeled and quartered
2 tablespoons finely crushed gingersnaps

In a large saucepan cook the meat in hot cooking oil till brown. Stir together the water, vinegar, dry onion soup mix, and bay leaf; pour the mixture over meat. Bring to boiling and reduce heat. Cover and simmer the meat mixture for 45 minutes.

Add the cabbage wedges and potato quarters to the meat mixture. Cover and simmer for 40 to 45 minutes more or till the meat and vegetables are tender. Transfer the cooked meat and vegetables to a serving platter and keep warm, reserving the pan juices.

For sauce, remove the bay leaf from the reserved pan juices and discard. Skim fat from the juices, if necessary. Stir the finely crushed gingersnaps into pan juices. Cook and stir till the mixture is thickened and bubbly.

To serve, spoon some of the warm sauce over the meat and vegetables. Pass any remaining sauce. Makes 2 servings.

Curried Beef and Broccoli

½ pound beef round steak
1 cup fresh broccoli
    buds *or* frozen cut
    broccoli
½ medium onion
½ cup beef broth
1 tablespoon all-purpose
    flour
1 teaspoon curry powder
¼ teaspoon salt
2 tablespoons cooking oil
    Chow mein noodles
    (optional)

Partially freeze steak; thinly slice meat across the grain into bite-size strips. Cut up any large fresh broccoli buds. (*Or*, thaw frozen cut broccoli.) Cut the onion into thin wedges. Set the meat and vegetables aside.

In a 2-cup glass measure or small mixing bowl stir together the beef broth, flour, curry powder, and salt; set aside.

Preheat a wok or skillet over high heat; add *1 tablespoon* of the cooking oil. Add broccoli and onion; stir-fry about 3 minutes or till broccoli is crisp-tender. Remove vegetables and set aside.

Add the remaining cooking oil to the hot wok or skillet. Add the beef strips; stir-fry for 2 minutes or till the meat is brown. Stir the broth mixture into the beef; cook and stir till the mixture is slightly thickened and bubbly. Return cooked vegetables to pan; cook and stir for 1 minute more or till heated through. Serve over chow mein noodles, if desired. Makes 2 servings.

Mexican Meat Loaf

1 slightly beaten egg
½ cup soft bread crumbs
2 tablespoons catsup
1 canned green chili
    pepper, rinsed,
    seeded, and chopped
    (about 2 tablespoons)
¼ teaspoon salt
¼ teaspoon chili powder
    Dash pepper
½ pound ground beef
2 tablespoons catsup
2 slices Monterey Jack
    cheese, quartered
    diagonally (1 ounce)

In a mixing bowl combine the egg, soft bread crumbs, 2 tablespoons catsup, chopped green chili pepper, salt, chili powder, and pepper. Add ground beef; mix well. Shape meat mixture into a 6x3-inch loaf. Place in a 9-inch pie plate. Bake the meat loaf in a 350° oven for 40 minutes. Drain off fat.

Spread 2 tablespoons catsup over the meat loaf. Arrange the cheese triangles atop. Return to oven and bake for 5 minutes more or till cheese is melted. Makes 2 servings.
• **Microwave directions:** Make the meat loaf as directed above. Place in a nonmetal 9-inch pie plate. Cover the pie plate with waxed paper and cook the meat loaf in a counter-top microwave oven on high power for 4 to 5 minutes or till meat is done, giving the dish a half-turn once during cooking. Drain off fat.

Spread 2 tablespoons catsup over the meat loaf and arrange the cheese triangles atop as directed above. Micro-cook the meat, uncovered, about 45 seconds more or till cheese is melted.

Carrot and Beef Patties

1 beaten egg
1 medium carrot, finely
    shredded (½ cup)
¼ teaspoon salt
    Dash pepper
½ pound ground beef
½ of a medium onion,
    sliced and separated
    into rings
½ cup sliced fresh
    mushrooms
1 tablespoon butter *or*
    margarine

In a mixing bowl combine the egg, shredded carrot, salt, and pepper. Add ground beef and mix well. Shape the meat mixture into two ¾-inch-thick patties.

In a skillet cook onion rings and mushroom slices in hot butter or margarine till the onion is tender but not brown. Remove onion rings and set aside.

In the same skillet cook patties about 10 minutes or to desired doneness, turning the patties once during cooking. To serve, garnish each patty with onion rings and mushrooms. Makes 2 servings.
• **Microwave directions:** Make the meat patties as directed above. Preheat the browning dish in a counter-top microwave oven for 5 minutes on high power. Add the patties, onion, and mushrooms, *omitting* the butter or margarine.

Cover the dish with a glass lid or waxed paper and micro-cook on high power for 2½ minutes. Turn the patties. Cover and micro-cook the patties for 2 minutes more or to desired doneness. Drain off fat. Serve as directed above.

Entrées–Meat

Baked Empanadas

½ pound ground beef
1 medium onion, chopped (½ cup)
1 clove garlic, minced
2 teaspoons all-purpose flour
¼ teaspoon salt
¼ to ½ teaspoon ground cumin
  Several dashes pepper
½ cup water
  Few dashes bottled hot pepper sauce
¼ cup chopped pimiento-stuffed olives
1 package (4) refrigerated crescent rolls
  Milk
  Sesame seed

For filling, in a skillet cook the ground beef, onion, and garlic till the meat is brown and onion is tender. Drain off fat. Stir in the flour, salt, cumin, and pepper. Add the water and hot pepper sauce all at once. Cook and stir till the mixture is thickened and bubbly. Cook and stir for 1 minute more. Stir in the chopped olives. Cool.

Separate crescent roll dough into 2 rectangles. Pinch perforations to seal. Roll *each* piece into a 7x4-inch rectangle (dough should be about ⅛ inch thick). Spoon *half* of the meat mixture onto the narrow end of *each* rectangle to within ½ inch of edge. Fold *each* rectangle of dough in half. Press the edges together with the tines of a fork to seal. Place filled fold-overs on an ungreased baking sheet. Prick tops 2 or 3 times with a fork. Brush with milk. Sprinkle with sesame seed. Bake in a 375° oven about 15 minutes or till golden brown. Makes 2 servings.

Cheese 'n' Burger Bundles

1 slightly beaten egg
1 tablespoon finely chopped onion
1 tablespoon fine dry bread crumbs
¼ teaspoon salt
  Dash pepper
½ pound ground beef, pork, lamb, *or* veal
1 tablespoon sweet pickle relish
1 tablespoon catsup
¼ cup shredded American cheese (1 ounce)

In a medium mixing bowl combine the beaten egg, chopped onion, dry bread crumbs, salt, and pepper. Add the ground beef, pork, lamb, or veal and mix well. Divide the meat mixture into 4 portions. Shape *each* portion of the meat mixture into a patty about 3½ inches in diameter. Set the 4 meat patties aside.

For filling, in a small mixing bowl stir together the sweet pickle relish and catsup. Spread *half* of the relish mixture atop *each* of 2 patties to within ¼ inch of edge. Top *each* of the 2 patties with *half* of the shredded American cheese. Top *each* with one of the remaining meat patties; pinch the edges of patties to seal.

Place the filled patties in a shallow baking dish. Bake patties, uncovered, in a 375° oven for 25 to 30 minutes or till done. Drain off fat. Makes 2 servings.

Pepper Beef Stir-Fry

6 ounces beef sirloin steak
3 tablespoons teriyaki sauce
2 tablespoons cognac *or* brandy
1½ teaspoons cornstarch
½ teaspoon grated gingerroot *or* ¼ teaspoon ground ginger
3 ounces fresh pea pods *or* ½ of a 6-ounce package frozen pea pods
1 tablespoon peanut oil *or* cooking oil
1 8-ounce can bamboo shoots, drained
½ of a red *or* green sweet pepper, cut into strips
  Hot cooked rice (optional)

Partially freeze steak; thinly slice the meat across the grain into bite-size strips.

For marinade, in a medium mixing bowl stir together the teriyaki sauce, cognac or brandy, cornstarch, and gingerroot or ground ginger. Add the steak strips; stir to coat. Marinate for 1 hour at room temperature.

Meanwhile, break off the fresh pea pods and remove strings. (Or, thaw frozen pea pods.)

Preheat wok or large skillet over high heat. Add peanut oil or cooking oil. Add meat and marinade; stir-fry about 5 minutes or just till meat is brown. Add the pea pods, bamboo shoots, and red or green sweet pepper strips. Cover and cook the mixture for 1 minute. Serve immediately with rice, if desired. Makes 2 servings.

Pictured opposite: Pepper Beef Stir-Fry

Entrées–Meat

Veal Parmigiana

    6 ounces boneless veal,
         cut into 2 pieces
    1 beaten egg
    2 teaspoons milk
    ¼ cup finely crushed
         saltine crackers
         (7 crackers)
    2 tablespoons grated
         Parmesan cheese
    2 tablespoons butter *or*
         margarine
    1 8-ounce can stewed
         tomatoes, cut up
    ¼ teaspoon dried oregano,
         crushed
         Dash pepper
    1 slice mozzarella cheese,
         cut into triangles
         (1 ounce)
         Grated Parmesan cheese
         (optional)

Place each piece of veal between 2 pieces of clear plastic wrap. Pound the veal with meat mallet to ¼-inch thickness, working from the center to edges. Remove the plastic wrap.

In a small mixing bowl stir together the beaten egg and the milk. In a shallow dish combine the crushed crackers and the 2 tablespoons Parmesan cheese. Dip the veal into the egg-milk mixture, then into the crumb mixture to coat evenly.

In a skillet cook veal in hot butter or margarine over high heat about 1 minute on each side or till brown. Transfer the veal to a heat-proof serving platter and keep warm.

In the same skillet combine *undrained* tomatoes, oregano, and pepper. Bring mixture to boiling; pour over veal. Top *each* piece of veal with 1 triangle of mozzarella cheese. Place under broiler. Broil just till cheese is melted. Sprinkle with Parmesan cheese, if desired. Makes 2 servings.

Spinach-Veal Rolls

    ½ pound boneless veal *or*
         boneless beef sirloin
         steak
    ½ of a 10-ounce package
         frozen chopped
         spinach, thawed
    2 tablespoons grated
         Parmesan cheese
    ¼ teaspoon dried basil,
         crushed
    3 tablespoons butter *or*
         margarine
    ½ teaspoon instant beef
         bouillon granules
    1 tablespoon all-purpose
         flour
    1 3-ounce can sliced
         mushrooms, drained
    2 tablespoons snipped
         parsley
         Hot cooked noodles

Cut veal or beef into 2 pieces. Place each piece of meat between 2 pieces of clear plastic wrap. Pound with a meat mallet to about a 5-inch square, working from center to edges. Remove plastic wrap; sprinkle with salt and pepper.

Squeeze excess water from the spinach. Stir in Parmesan cheese and basil. Spoon *half* of the spinach mixture onto *each* piece of meat. Roll up, securing rolls with wooden picks. In a skillet cook meat rolls in hot butter or margarine over medium heat about 8 minutes or till brown on all sides. Add the bouillon granules and ¾ cup *water*. Bring to boiling; reduce heat. Cover and simmer for 45 to 60 minutes or till tender. Remove meat and keep warm, reserving cooking liquid.

For sauce, skim fat from cooking liquid. Measure liquid; add water, if necessary, to make ⅔ cup. Stir together flour and 2 tablespoons *water;* stir into liquid. Cook and stir till thickened and bubbly. Cook and stir for 1 minute more. Stir in mushrooms and parsley. Heat through. Serve over meat and noodles. Makes 2 servings.

Orange Lamb Shanks

If your butcher doesn't have lamb shanks, you can easily substitute beef short ribs in this spicy dish—

    2 lamb shanks (about 12
         ounces each) *or* 1½ to
         2 pounds beef short
         ribs
    2 tablespoons cooking oil
         Salt
         Pepper
    2 teaspoons finely
         shredded orange peel
    ¾ cup orange juice
    2 tablespoons teriyaki
         sauce
    1 clove garlic, minced
    1 teaspoon curry powder
         Hot cooked rice
         Quartered orange slices
         (optional)
         Snipped parsley
         (optional)

In a 10-inch skillet or a 3-quart saucepan cook the lamb shanks or beef short ribs in hot cooking oil till brown on all sides. Sprinkle the meat with salt and pepper. Drain off fat.

In a mixing bowl combine the shredded orange peel, the orange juice, teriyaki sauce, minced garlic, and curry powder; pour over the meat. Bring to boiling; reduce heat. Cover and simmer for 1 to 1¼ hours or till the meat is tender, turning occasionally.

Skim the fat from pan juices. Serve the meat and pan juices over hot cooked rice. Garnish the meat with the quartered orange slices and snipped fresh parsley, if desired. Makes 2 servings.

Curried Lamb Meatballs

1 beaten egg
1 tablespoon milk
½ cup soft bread crumbs
¼ teaspoon salt
⅛ teaspoon dried oregano, crushed
6 ounces ground lamb
¼ cup chopped onion
½ to 1 teaspoon curry powder
1 tablespoon butter *or* margarine
1 tablespoon all-purpose flour
1 teaspoon instant chicken bouillon granules
⅛ teaspoon salt
⅛ teaspoon paprika
Dash pepper
¾ cup water
1 small apple, peeled and chopped
Hot cooked rice (optional)
Chopped salted peanuts (optional)
Chutney (optional)

In a mixing bowl combine the beaten egg and milk. Stir in the bread crumbs, the ¼ teaspoon salt, and oregano. Add the ground lamb; mix well. Shape into 8 meatballs about ½ inch in diameter. Place in shallow baking pan. Bake in a 375° oven for 20 to 25 minutes.

In a skillet cook the onion and curry powder in hot butter or margarine till onion is tender but not brown. Stir in the flour, chicken bouillon granules, the ⅛ teaspoon salt, the paprika, and pepper. Stir in the water all at once. Cook and stir till thickened and bubbly. Cook and stir for 1 minute more.

Stir the meatballs into the curry mixture. Cover and cook over low heat for 10 minutes. Stir in the chopped apple. Cover and cook for 2 minutes more. Serve with hot cooked rice, chopped salted peanuts, or chutney, if desired. Makes 2 servings.

Pear and Pork Stir-Fry

½ pound boneless pork
1 teaspoon cornstarch
1 teaspoon brown sugar
½ teaspoon instant chicken bouillon granules
¼ teaspoon ground ginger
¼ cup pear nectar *or* water
1 tablespoon soy sauce
1 teaspoon white wine vinegar
1 tablespoon cooking oil
1 small green pepper, seeded and cut into ¾-inch pieces
1 firm large pear *or* apple, peeled, cored, and sliced into bite-size pieces (1 cup)
2 tablespoons cashews *or* peanuts

Partially freeze pork; thinly slice the meat across the grain into bite-size strips.

In a small mixing bowl combine the cornstarch, brown sugar, bouillon granules, and ginger. Stir in the pear nectar or water, soy sauce, and white wine vinegar; set aside.

Preheat wok or large skillet over high heat; add cooking oil. Add green pepper; stir-fry in hot oil about 2 minutes. Remove from wok. Add pork to wok or skillet and stir-fry for 2 to 3 minutes.

Stir the soy sauce mixture; stir into pork. Cook and stir till the mixture is thickened and bubbly. Stir in the cooked green pepper, sliced pear or apple, and the cashews or peanuts. Cover and cook for 3 minutes more. Serve immediately. Makes 2 servings.

Cheesy Liver and Broccoli Bake

½ of a 10-ounce package frozen cut broccoli
6 to 8 ounces sliced beef liver, cut ½ inch thick
4 teaspoons all-purpose flour
¼ cup butter *or* margarine
½ cup sliced fresh mushrooms
¼ cup bias-sliced green onion
1 tablespoon all-purpose flour
¾ cup milk
¼ cup shredded process Swiss *or* American cheese
2 tablespoons fine dry bread crumbs
2 tablespoons grated Parmesan cheese
1 tablespoon snipped parsley

Cook broccoli according to package directions; drain and set aside. Cut liver into strips; sprinkle with salt and pepper. Coat with the 4 teaspoons flour. Cook liver in *1 tablespoon* of hot butter for 4 to 5 minutes or till brown. Remove; set aside. Cook mushrooms and onion in *1 tablespoon* of hot butter till tender. Remove; set aside.

Melt *1 tablespoon* of the butter. Stir in the 1 tablespoon flour, ⅛ teaspoon *salt,* and a dash *pepper.* Add milk all at once. Cook and stir till thickened and bubbly. Cook and stir for 1 minute more. Add cheese; stir till melted. Stir broccoli into ½ *cup* of the cheese sauce; set aside remaining sauce.

Pour broccoli mixture into an 8x6x2-inch baking dish; top with the liver, mushrooms, and onions. Pour remaining sauce atop.

Melt the remaining butter; stir in bread crumbs, Parmesan cheese, and parsley. Sprinkle crumb mixture over sauce. Bake in a 350° oven for 15 to 20 minutes or till heated through. Makes 2 servings.

Entrées–Meat

Creamy Ham in Caraway Puffs

2 tablespoons butter *or* margarine
¼ cup water
¼ cup all-purpose flour
Dash salt
1 egg
½ teaspoon caraway seed
1 tablespoon butter *or* margarine
1 tablespoon all-purpose flour
¼ teaspoon dry mustard
⅛ teaspoon salt
Dash pepper
¾ cup milk
½ cup cubed fully cooked ham
2 hard-cooked eggs, sliced
2 tablespoons chopped green pepper
1 teaspoon chopped pimiento

In a medium saucepan melt the 2 tablespoons butter or margarine. Add the water; bring to boiling. Add the ¼ cup flour and the dash salt all at once; stir vigorously. Cook and stir till mixture forms a ball that doesn't separate. Remove from heat and cool slightly (about 5 minutes). Add the egg, beating with a wooden spoon till smooth. Stir in caraway seed.

Drop batter in 2 portions, 3 inches apart, onto a greased baking sheet. Bake in a 450° oven for 15 minutes. Reduce heat to 325°; bake 25 minutes more. Remove puffs from oven; cool. Slice off tops and remove any soft dough inside. Cool on a wire rack.

For filling, melt the 1 tablespoon butter or margarine in saucepan; stir in the 1 tablespoon flour, dry mustard, the ⅛ teaspoon salt, and the pepper. Add milk. Cook and stir till thickened and bubbly. Cook and stir for 1 minute more. Stir in ham, sliced eggs, green pepper, and pimiento; heat through. Spoon mixture into puffs; serve immediately. Makes 2 servings.

Broccoli and Ham Roll-Ups

1 10-ounce package frozen broccoli spears
1 8-ounce can pineapple slices (juice pack)
1½ teaspoons butter *or* margarine
1½ teaspoons all-purpose flour
1½ teaspoons prepared horseradish
1 teaspoon prepared mustard
¼ teaspoon grated onion
¼ teaspoon Worcestershire sauce
⅛ teaspoon salt
¼ cup milk
1 slightly beaten egg yolk
4 slices boiled ham
2 slices process Swiss cheese

Cook broccoli according to package directions; drain. Drain pineapple, reserving ½ cup juice. Set pineapple slices aside.

Meanwhile, in a saucepan melt butter or margarine. Stir in the flour, horseradish, mustard, onion, Worcestershire sauce, and salt. Add milk all at once. Cook and stir till thickened and bubbly. Cook and stir for 1 minute more. Combine the egg yolk and reserved pineapple juice. Add *half* of the hot mixture to egg yolk mixture. Return all to pan. Cook and stir over low heat till thickened.

For each roll-up, top *two* ham slices with *one* slice of cheese. Place *half* of the cooked broccoli on each. Spoon *1 tablespoon* of the sauce over broccoli; set aside remaining sauce. Roll ham and cheese around broccoli; secure with wooden picks. Place roll-ups in a shallow baking dish. Cover and bake in a 350° oven about 25 minutes or till heated through.

Reheat and pass the remaining sauce. Garnish with the pineapple slices. Makes 2 servings.

Fried Rice with Ham

1 tablespoon butter *or* margarine
½ cup sliced fresh mushrooms
2 tablespoons cooking oil
1½ cups cooked long grain rice, chilled
2 green onions, sliced into long thin shreds
½ cup diced fully cooked ham
½ cup fresh bean sprouts
¼ cup finely chopped onion
2 tablespoons finely chopped green pepper
½ teaspoon grated gingerroot
1 tablespoon soy sauce
½ teaspoon light Scotch whisky (optional)
¼ teaspoon salt
Dash pepper
2 beaten eggs
Soy sauce (optional)

Preheat a wok or large skillet over low heat; add butter or margarine. Cook mushrooms in hot butter or margarine till tender; remove.

Heat wok or skillet over high heat; add the cooking oil. Add the rice and stir-fry for 2 minutes. Add the green onion; stir-fry with rice 1 minute. Add the mushrooms, ham, bean sprouts, onion, green pepper, and gingerroot. Stir-fry for 2 minutes. Stir in the soy sauce, Scotch if desired, salt, and pepper. Reduce heat to medium.

Push the rice mixture into a ring around sides of wok, leaving a well in center. Pour in the beaten eggs. Cook, without stirring, for 1 minute or till eggs begin to set on bottom and around edges. With a spatula, lift and fold eggs so the uncooked portion flows underneath. Continue cooking over medium heat till eggs are cooked throughout. Toss the rice mixture with the eggs for 1 minute. Serve immediately. Pass additional soy sauce, if desired. Makes 2 servings.

Chutney Spareribs

1½ to 2 pounds pork spareribs
    Salt
    Pepper
½ cup chopped chutney
2 tablespoons chili sauce
1½ teaspoons vinegar
1 teaspoon Worcestershire sauce
½ teaspoon onion salt
¼ teaspoon dry mustard
    Dash bottled hot pepper sauce

Sprinkle ribs with salt and pepper. Place ribs, meaty side down, in a shallow roasting pan. Roast in a 450° oven for 30 minutes. Remove meat from oven; drain off fat. Turn ribs meaty side up. Reduce oven temperature to 350° and continue roasting for 30 minutes more.

Meanwhile, for sauce, in a small mixing bowl combine the chutney, chili sauce, vinegar, the Worcestershire sauce, onion salt, mustard, and hot pepper sauce.

Brush meat with *some* of the chutney sauce. Roast for 30 minutes more or till tender, brushing with sauce frequently. Heat the remaining sauce to pass with the ribs. Makes 2 servings.

• **Barbecue directions:** In a large covered saucepan cook the ribs in enough boiling salted water to cover for 45 to 60 minutes or till ribs are tender. Drain well; sprinkle the ribs with salt and pepper.

Prepare the sauce as directed above. Brush *some* of the sauce over ribs. Grill the ribs over *medium-slow* coals for 10 to 15 minutes. Turn and grill for 10 to 15 minutes more or till tender, brushing occasionally with sauce. Heat remaining sauce to pass.

Peach-Glazed Ribs

1 pound pork country-style ribs
1 tablespoon cooking oil
¼ cup peach preserves
¼ cup beef broth
1 tablespoon vinegar
2 teaspoons Worcestershire sauce
½ teaspoon salt
1 small onion, thinly sliced
¼ cup cold water
1 tablespoon all-purpose flour
    Hot cooked noodles

Trim fat from ribs. In a 2-quart saucepan; cook the ribs in hot cooking oil till brown on all sides. Drain off fat. Sprinkle ribs with salt and pepper.

In a mixing bowl combine the peach preserves, beef broth, vinegar, Worcestershire sauce, and salt; pour over meat. Place onion atop meat. Bring to boiling; reduce heat. Cover and simmer for 1¼ to 1½ hours or till ribs are tender. Transfer the ribs to a serving platter, reserving the cooking liquid; keep ribs warm.

For sauce, skim fat from reserved cooking liquid. Stir together the water and flour; stir into cooking liquid. Cook and stir till thickened and bubbly. Cook and stir for 1 minute more. Serve the sauce over the ribs and hot cooked noodles. Makes 2 servings.

• **Crockery cooker directions:** In a small mixing bowl combine the peach preserves, beef broth, vinegar, Worcestershire sauce, and salt. Place ribs in a 4-cup electric slow crockery cooker, *omitting* oil. Place the onion atop meat; pour the broth mixture atop. Cover and cook on low-heat setting for 8 hours. Transfer the ribs and onion to a serving platter, reserving the cooking liquid; keep ribs warm.

Skim the fat from cooking liquid. Make the sauce and serve over the ribs and hot noodles as above.

Tortilla-Topped Pork Chops

Adjust the level of chili powder to suit your own taste—

2 pork chops, cut ½ inch thick
1 tablespoon cooking oil
    Salt
    Pepper
1 8-ounce can vegetarian beans in tomato sauce
1 tablespoon diced dried bell pepper
1 teaspoon minced dried onion
½ teaspoon chili powder
    Dash ground cinnamon
    Dash ground cloves
    Coarsely crushed tortilla chips *or* corn chips
    Dairy sour cream (optional)

Trim the fat from chops; discard trimmings. In a skillet cook the pork chops on both sides in hot cooking oil till brown. Sprinkle the chops with salt and pepper.

Meanwhile, in a 7-inch pie plate combine the vegetarian beans in tomato sauce, dried bell pepper, minced dried onion, chili powder, cinnamon, and cloves.

Arrange the 2 chops atop the bean mixture in the pie plate. Cover with foil and bake in a 350° oven about 50 minutes or till the meat is tender.

Sprinkle the baked pork chops and beans with coarsely crushed tortilla chips or corn chips before serving. Top each serving with a dollop of sour cream, if desired. Makes 2 servings.

Entrées–Meat

Bulgur-Stuffed Chops

2 pork chops *or* **4 lamb chops, cut 1 inch thick**
⅓ cup water
¼ cup shredded carrot
2 tablespoons bulgur wheat
2 tablespoons chopped onion
⅛ teaspoon salt
2 tablespoons chopped cashews
1 tablespoon snipped parsley *or* **1 teaspoon snipped mint**
Salt
Pepper
Fresh parsley *or* **mint (optional)**

Using a sharp paring knife, make a pocket in each chop, cutting from the fat side almost to the bone (step 1).

For stuffing, in a small saucepan combine the water, carrot, bulgur wheat, onion, and the ⅛ teaspoon salt. Cover and simmer for 20 to 25 minutes or till the vegetables and bulgur are tender. Stir in the cashews and the 1 tablespoon parsley or the 1 teaspoon mint.

Spoon an equal amount of the bulgur stuffing into the pocket of each chop (step 2). Skewer with wooden picks, if desired. Place the meat on rack of unheated broiler pan. Broil the stuffed chops 2 to 3 inches from heat for 10 to 12 minutes for pork or 7 to 8 minutes for lamb. Sprinkle with salt and pepper. Turn meat. Broil 10 to 12 minutes more for pork or 7 to 8 minutes more for lamb. Sprinkle with salt and pepper. Garnish the chops with the parsley or mint, if desired. Makes 2 servings.

1 *To make a pocket in the chop, first cut a 1½- to 2-inch-long slit in the fatty side of the chop. Then, insert the knife into the slit as shown, drawing the knife from side to side to form a larger pocket inside the chop. Cut almost to the bone edge, trying not to make the initial slit any larger when forming the pocket (so the chop will be easier to close when it is stuffed). Repeat with the remaining chop(s).*

2 *Using a teaspoon, carefully spoon equal amounts of the stuffing mixture into the pocket of each chop as shown.*

If desired, to ensure that the stuffing stays inside the meat pockets while baking, carefully insert two wooden picks into the chops diagonally to close the pockets. Remove the wooden picks before serving.

Polish Sausage and Peppers

Substitute mild Italian sausage for the Polish sausage, if you prefer—

½ **pound Polish sausage links, bias-sliced into ½-inch slices**
1 **small onion, coarsely chopped**
1 **small clove garlic, minced**
1 **7½-ounce can tomatoes, cut up**
1 **medium green *or* red sweet pepper, coarsely chopped**
2 **tablespoons water**
1 **tablespoon snipped fresh basil *or* 1 teaspoon dried basil, crushed**
¼ **teaspoon lemon pepper Hot cooked rice**

In a medium skillet cook the Polish sausage slices till brown. Remove sausage from pan and drain on paper toweling, reserving the pan drippings.

To the reserved drippings in the skillet add the chopped onion and minced garlic; cook about 5 minutes or till onion is tender but not brown. Drain off fat.

Stir *undrained* tomatoes, green or red sweet pepper, water, basil, and lemon pepper into the skillet. Return the browned Polish sausage slices to the skillet. Bring the mixture to boiling and reduce heat. Cook, uncovered, over low heat for 30 minutes, stirring occasionally. To serve, spoon the sausage-pepper mixture over hot cooked rice. Makes 2 servings.

Frankfurter and Olive Pizza

⅔ **cup all-purpose flour**
½ **teaspoon baking powder Dash salt Dash garlic powder**
¼ **cup milk**
1 **tablespoon cooking oil**
¼ **cup pizza sauce**
¼ **teaspoon dried oregano, crushed**
3 **frankfurters, cut into ½-inch slices, *or* ¼ pound salami, cut up**
¼ **cup sliced pitted ripe olives *or* canned sliced mushrooms**
½ **cup shredded American cheese *or* shredded mozzarella cheese**

For dough, in a mixing bowl stir together the flour, baking powder, salt, and garlic powder. Combine the milk and cooking oil. Make a well in the center of the dry ingredients; add the milk mixture all at once. Stir just till the dough clings together.

Knead dough gently on a lightly floured surface for 10 strokes. Roll or pat the dough into a circle 8 inches in diameter. Place dough on a greased baking sheet, building up a ½-inch edge.

Spread the pizza sauce over the dough; sprinkle with oregano. Top with the frankfurter or the salami pieces and the sliced olives or mushrooms. Sprinkle the shredded American or the mozzarella cheese atop. Bake the pizza in a 450° oven for 12 to 15 minutes. Makes 2 servings.

Franks and Corn Casserole

4 **frankfurters**
2 **ounces cheddar cheese, cut into 4 strips (3x¾x¼ inches)**
2 **tablespoons chopped onion**
2 **tablespoons chopped green pepper**
1 **tablespoon butter *or* margarine**
1 **8½-ounce can cream-style corn**
½ **of a 3-ounce package cream cheese**
1 **tablespoon chopped pimiento**
½ **teaspoon ground coriander**
⅓ **cup coarsely crushed corn chips**

Cut frankfurters lengthwise almost through to opposite side. Place a cheese strip in the center of each split frankfurter. Place the cheese-stuffed frankfurters, cheese side up, in an ungreased 8x6½x2-inch baking dish.

In a small saucepan cook the onion and green pepper in hot butter or margarine till tender but not brown. Stir in the corn, cream cheese, pimiento, and coriander. Cook and stir over low heat till the cream cheese is melted and the mixture is combined.

Pour the corn mixture over the stuffed frankfurters in the baking dish. Sprinkle with the crushed corn chips. Bake, uncovered, in a 350° oven about 30 minutes or till frankfurters are heated through. Makes 2 servings.

Entrées-Poultry

Marengo-Style Chicken

- 4 chicken drumsticks *or* chicken thighs *or* 2 chicken legs *or* 1 whole medium chicken breast, halved lengthwise
- 1 tablespoon butter *or* margarine
- ¼ cup chopped onion
- ¼ cup chopped green pepper
- 1 7½-ounce can tomatoes, cut up
- ½ cup tomato juice
- 2 tablespoons sliced pimiento-stuffed olives
- ½ teaspoon dried basil, crushed
- ⅛ teaspoon salt
- ⅛ teaspoon garlic powder
- ⅛ teaspoon ground cumin
  Dash chili powder
- 2 tablespoons raisins
- ⅓ cup brown rice

Rinse chicken pieces in cold water; pat dry with paper toweling. In a skillet cook chicken pieces in hot butter or margarine about 15 minutes or till brown, turning pieces once. Remove the chicken pieces, reserving drippings; set chicken aside. To the reserved drippings in skillet add the onion and green pepper; cook till tender but not brown. Drain off fat. Return the chicken pieces to skillet.

Combine *undrained* tomatoes, tomato juice, olives, basil, salt, garlic powder, cumin, and chili powder. Pour over chicken. Bring to boiling; reduce heat. Cover and simmer for 25 minutes or till chicken is tender. Add raisins and simmer, uncovered, for 10 minutes more. Skim off fat.

Meanwhile, cook the brown rice according to package directions. Serve chicken and sauce over rice. Makes 2 servings.

Chicken Fricassee with Lemon Dumplings

- 4 chicken drumsticks *or* chicken thighs *or* 2 chicken legs *or* 1 whole medium chicken breast, halved lengthwise
- 1 cup water
- ¼ cup chopped celery
- 1 tablespoon chopped onion
- 1 teaspoon instant chicken bouillon granules
- ½ teaspoon salt
  Dash pepper
- ½ cup cold water
- 3 tablespoons all-purpose flour
- ½ of a 10-ounce package frozen mixed vegetables (about 1 cup)
  Lemon Dumplings

Rinse the chicken pieces in cold water. In a 2-quart saucepan combine the chicken pieces, the 1 cup water, the celery, onion, bouillon granules, salt, and pepper. Bring to boiling; reduce heat. Cover and simmer for 20 minutes.

Stir together the ½ cup water and the flour; stir into chicken mixture. Cook and stir over medium heat till thickened and bubbly. Stir in vegetables.

Prepare the Lemon Dumplings. Drop dough from a tablespoon to make 4 mounds atop the bubbling chicken mixture. Simmer dumplings, uncovered, for 10 minutes. Cover and simmer for 10 minutes more (do not lift cover). Makes 2 servings.

• **Lemon Dumplings:** In a mixing bowl place ¾ cup *packaged biscuit mix*. Make a well in center. Add ¼ cup *milk* all at once. Add ½ teaspoon finely shredded *lemon peel* and 1 teaspoon *lemon juice*. Stir just till dough clings together.

Chicken with Mushrooms

- 4 chicken thighs *or* 1 whole medium chicken breast, halved lengthwise
- 2 tablespoons all-purpose flour
- ⅛ teaspoon salt
  Dash pepper
- 1 tablespoon cooking oil *or* shortening
- ¾ cup sliced fresh mushrooms
- ⅓ cup dry white wine
- 2 tablespoons sliced green onion
- 1 small clove garlic, minced
- 1 teaspoon snipped fresh tarragon *or* ¼ teaspoon dried tarragon, crushed
- 1 tablespoon snipped parsley

Rinse chicken pieces in cold water; pat dry with paper toweling. In a paper or plastic bag combine the flour, salt, and pepper. Add the chicken pieces; shake to coat. In an 8-inch skillet cook chicken in hot cooking oil or shortening about 15 minutes or till brown, turning once. Drain off fat.

Add sliced mushrooms, white wine, green onion, garlic, and tarragon to skillet. Bring to boiling; reduce heat. Cover and simmer for 30 to 35 minutes or till the chicken is tender.

To serve, spoon *some* of the sauce over the chicken; sprinkle with parsley. Pass the remaining sauce. Makes 2 servings.

53

Monterey Chicken Rolls

1 whole medium chicken
  breast, skinned,
  halved lengthwise, and
  boned
  Salt
  Pepper
½ ounce Monterey Jack
  cheese, cut into 2
  pieces (¾x½x½
  inches each)
1 tablespoon all-purpose
  flour
1 beaten egg
2 tablespoons fine dry
  bread crumbs
2 tablespoons dry white
  wine
1 tablespoon butter or
  margarine, softened
1 teaspoon snipped
  parsley
⅛ teaspoon dried oregano,
  crushed, or dried
  marjoram, crushed

Place *each* piece of the chicken, boned side up, between 2 pieces of clear plastic wrap. Working from center to edges, pound lightly with a meat mallet, forming 2 rectangles about ⅛ inch thick. Remove plastic wrap. Sprinkle with salt and pepper.

Place *one* piece of cheese onto *each* piece of chicken. Fold in sides; roll up jelly-roll style. Skewer closed with wooden picks. Roll chicken in flour, then dip in beaten egg. Roll in fine dry bread crumbs to coat evenly.

Place chicken rolls, seam side down, in a shallow baking dish. Bake, uncovered, in a 350° oven for 30 minutes.

Meanwhile, for sauce, in a small saucepan combine the white wine, butter or margarine, parsley, and oregano or marjoram. Cook and stir over low heat till butter or margarine is melted. Pour the sauce over chicken rolls; continue baking about 10 minutes or till tender. Remove the wooden picks before serving. Makes 2 servings.

Paprikas Chicken

4 chicken drumsticks or
  chicken thighs or 2
  chicken legs or 1 whole
  medium chicken
  breast, halved
  lengthwise
1 medium onion, chopped
  (½ cup)
¼ cup chopped green
  pepper
2 tablespoons cooking oil
2 tablespoons paprika
½ cup water
½ teaspoon salt
  Dash pepper
¼ cup dairy sour cream
1 tablespoon all-purpose
  flour
  Hot cooked noodles

Rinse chicken pieces in cold water; pat dry with paper toweling. In a skillet cook onion and green pepper in hot oil till tender but not brown. Remove from heat; stir in paprika till combined.

Add chicken to paprika mixture, turning the pieces to coat evenly. Cook over low heat about 5 minutes, stirring constantly so the paprika does not burn. Add water, salt, and pepper. Bring to boiling; reduce heat. Cover and simmer about 40 minutes or till the chicken is tender. Remove skillet from heat. Remove the chicken pieces, reserving cooking liquid; set chicken aside.

Skim fat from reserved cooking liquid. Pour the liquid into a blender container; cover and blend till the mixture is smooth. Add enough water to blended mixture to measure 1 cup. Stir together the sour cream and flour; stir into blended mixture.

Return blended mixture to skillet. Cook and stir till thickened and bubbly. Cook and stir for 1 minute more. Add chicken pieces; heat through over low heat. Serve over the hot cooked noodles. Makes 2 servings.

Boning a Chicken Breast

Split the chicken breast in half lengthwise. Hold *one* of the halves bone side down. Starting from the breastbone side, cut meat away from the bone as close to the bone as possible. Press the flat side of the knife blade against the rib bones, gently pulling meat up and away from the bones as you cut. Repeat with remaining chicken breast half.

Tangy Chicken

4 chicken drumsticks or
  chicken thighs or 2
  chicken legs or 1
  whole medium
  chicken breast,
  halved lengthwise
  Cooking oil
¼ cup French salad
  dressing
1 teaspoon Worcestershire
  sauce
⅛ teaspoon celery seed

Rinse chicken; pat dry. Brush with oil; sprinkle with salt and pepper.

For sauce, combine the French salad dressing, the Worcestershire sauce, and celery seed.

Place chicken, skin side up, on rack of unheated broiler pan. Broil 5 to 6 inches from heat for 20 minutes. Turn pieces and broil about 15 minutes more or till tender. Brush often with sauce during last 5 minutes. (Or, grill chicken over *medium-hot* coals for 25 minutes, turning pieces occasionally. Brush with sauce. Grill about 15 minutes more or till tender, brushing often with sauce.) Makes 2 servings.

Entrées-Poultry & Seafood

Stir-Fried Chicken and Cashews

Hoisin sauce is a fermented soybean product often used in the Orient. If you don't have it on hand, simply substitute equal parts of brown sugar and soy sauce with a dash of garlic powder—

- 1 **whole medium chicken breast, skinned, boned, and cut into ½-inch pieces**
- 1 **tablespoon dry sherry**
- 1 **tablespoon soy sauce**
- ¼ **teaspoon sugar (optional)**
- 1 **tablespoon cooking oil**
- ½ **cup cashews**
- 1½ **teaspoons hoisin sauce**
  Sliced green onion (optional)
  Green onion fans (optional)
  Hot cooked rice

In a medium mixing bowl combine the chicken pieces, dry sherry, soy sauce, and sugar if desired; set aside.

Preheat a wok or skillet over high heat; add the cooking oil. Add cashews; stir-fry for 1 to 2 minutes or till cashews are brown. Remove cashews from wok or skillet; set aside. Add the chicken mixture to the wok or skillet; stir-fry for 2 to 3 minutes or just till chicken is done. Stir the hoisin sauce and the cashews into the chicken mixture.

If desired, sprinkle with sliced green onion and garnish with the green onion fans. Serve immediately with hot cooked rice. Makes 2 servings.

Granola-Stuffed Cornish Hen

(pictured on page 56)

- 1 **1- to 1½-pound Cornish game hen**
- ¼ **cup chopped onion**
- 1 **tablespoon butter *or* margarine**
- ½ **cup cooked rice**
- ½ **cup granola**
- ¼ **cup raisins**
- ½ **teaspoon finely shredded orange peel (set aside)**
- 1 **tablespoon orange juice**
- ¼ **teaspoon salt**
- ¼ **teaspoon curry powder**
- 1 **teaspoon cornstarch**
- 1 **teaspoon brown sugar**
- ¼ **teaspoon instant chicken bouillon granules**
- ⅓ **cup water**
- ¼ **cup orange juice**

Have a butcher halve the Cornish hen lengthwise. Rinse hen in cold water. Pat dry with paper toweling.

For stuffing, in a saucepan cook onion in hot butter or margarine till tender but not brown. Stir in rice, granola, raisins, the 1 tablespoon orange juice, salt, and curry powder. Toss gently to mix.

In a 1½-quart casserole or 9-inch pie plate, spoon the stuffing into 2 mounds. Place *each* hen half, cut side down, over a mound of stuffing. Bake, uncovered, in a 350° oven for 50 to 60 minutes or till the hen is done.

For sauce, in a small saucepan combine cornstarch, brown sugar, and bouillon granules. Stir in the water, the ¼ cup orange juice, and shredded orange peel. Cook and stir till thickened and bubbly. Cook and stir for 2 minutes more.

To serve, carefully transfer the hen halves and the stuffing to plates, keeping stuffing intact under each hen half. Spoon *some* of the sauce over the hen halves; pass the remaining sauce. Makes 2 servings.

Chicken Liver Stroganoff

- 2 **slices bacon**
- ¾ **cup sliced fresh mushrooms**
- ¼ **cup chopped onion**
- 8 **ounces chicken livers, cut up**
- ¼ **teaspoon instant chicken bouillon granules**
- ¼ **cup hot water**
- ½ **cup dairy sour cream**
- 1 **tablespoon all-purpose flour**
- 2 **tablespoons dry sherry**
  Hot cooked noodles
  Snipped parsley (optional)

In an 8-inch skillet cook bacon till crisp. Remove bacon and drain on paper toweling, reserving 1 tablespoon drippings in skillet. Crumble the bacon and set aside.

Cook the sliced mushrooms and chopped onion in the reserved drippings till tender but not brown. Add the chicken livers; cook 5 to 6 minutes or just till slightly pink in the center.

In a small mixing bowl dissolve bouillon granules in hot water. Stir together sour cream and flour. Gradually stir *some* of the bouillon mixture into the sour cream mixture. Return all to the mixing bowl. Stir in the sherry.

Add the sour cream mixture to the liver mixture in the skillet. Cook and stir till thickened and bubbly. Cook and stir for 1 minute more. Serve the liver mixture over hot cooked noodles; garnish with the crumbled bacon. Sprinkle with the snipped parsley, if desired. Makes 2 servings.

Deviled Fish Kabobs

- 8 ounces frozen fish fillets
- 1 8-ounce can pineapple chunks (juice pack)
- 2 tablespoons chopped onion
- 2 tablespoons soy sauce
- 1 tablespoon brown sugar
- 1 tablespoon cooking oil
- 1 clove garlic, minced
- ½ teaspoon dry mustard
  Dash bottled hot pepper sauce
- 2 medium carrots, bias-sliced into 2-inch pieces

Let fish thaw at room temperature for 30 minutes. Drain pineapple, reserving ¼ cup juice; set the pineapple chunks aside.

For marinade, in a saucepan combine the reserved pineapple juice, chopped onion, soy sauce, brown sugar, cooking oil, garlic, mustard, and hot pepper sauce. Bring to boiling; reduce heat. Simmer, uncovered, for 5 minutes; let the marinade cool.

Cut the fish fillets into 1½-inch pieces; place in a shallow baking dish. Pour the marinade over fish. Let stand at room temperature for 30 minutes, gently stirring once to distribute marinade.

Meanwhile, cook carrot slices, uncovered, in a small amount of boiling salted water for 15 to 20 minutes or till tender; drain.

Drain the fish, reserving marinade. On 2 long skewers alternately thread the fish, carrots, and pineapple. Place the kabobs on a greased grill and grill over *medium* coals for 8 to 10 minutes or till done, turning occasionally. *(Or,* place fish kabobs on a greased rack of unheated broiler pan. Broil 4 to 5 inches from heat for 8 to 10 minutes or till done, turning once.)

Heat reserved marinade; pass with kabobs. Makes 2 servings.

Salmon Tart

- Pastry for 7-inch Single-Crust Pie
- ¼ cup chopped celery
- 1 tablespoon chopped green onion
- 1 tablespoon butter *or* margarine
- 1 beaten egg
- ½ cup light cream *or* milk
- 1 teaspoon all-purpose flour
- ¼ teaspoon ground coriander
- 1 7¾-ounce can salmon, drained, flaked, and skin and bones removed, *or* one 6½-ounce can tuna, drained and flaked
- Paprika

Prepare Pastry for 7-inch Single-Crust Pie; roll into a circle 10 inches in diameter. Line a 7-inch pie plate with the pastry. Flute edge; prick bottom and sides with a fork. Bake the pastry in a 425° oven for 7 to 9 minutes or till golden.

Meanwhile, in a skillet cook the celery and green onion in hot butter or margarine till the onion is tender but not brown.

In a mixing bowl combine the beaten egg, cream or milk, flour, and coriander. Stir in the celery, green onion, and salmon or tuna.

Pour the fish mixture into the hot pastry shell. Sprinkle with paprika. If necessary, cover the edge of crust with foil to prevent over-browning. Bake in a 325° oven for 30 to 35 minutes or till a knife inserted near the center comes out clean. Let stand 5 minutes before serving. Makes 2 servings.

• **Pastry for 7-inch Single-Crust Pie:** Stir together ½ cup *all-purpose flour* and ¼ teaspoon *salt.* Cut in 3 tablespoons *shortening* till pieces are the size of small peas. Sprinkle 1 tablespoon *cold water* over part of the mixture; gently toss with a fork. Push to side of bowl. Repeat with another 1 to 2 teaspoons *cold water* till all is moistened. Form the dough into a ball.

Scallops Mornay

- 8 ounces fresh *or* frozen scallops
- 2 frozen patty shells
- ¾ cup water
- ½ cup frozen peas
- ¼ cup dry sherry
- ¼ teaspoon minced dried onion
  Dash pepper
- 1 cup sliced fresh mushrooms
- 1 tablespoon butter *or* margarine
- 4 teaspoons all-purpose flour
- ⅓ cup milk
- ¼ cup shredded *process* Swiss cheese

Thaw scallops, if frozen. Cut any large scallops into halves or quarters. Bake patty shells according to package directions.

In saucepan combine the water, peas, dry sherry, onion, and pepper. Bring to boiling; reduce heat. Cover and simmer for 5 minutes. Add the scallops and sliced mushrooms. Return to boiling; reduce heat. Cover and simmer for 1 to 2 minutes or till scallops are done. Remove the scallops, peas, and mushrooms with a slotted spoon, reserving cooking liquid; set the scallops and vegetables aside.

For sauce, bring the reserved cooking liquid to boiling and cook, uncovered, till liquid is reduced to ⅓ cup. In another saucepan melt the butter or margarine; stir in the flour. Stir in reduced cooking liquid and the milk. Cook and stir till mixture is thickened and bubbly. Cook and stir for 1 minute more. Reduce heat. Add the shredded cheese, stirring till cheese is melted. Stir in scallops, peas, and mushrooms. Heat through. Serve the scallop mixture in the baked patty shells. Makes 2 servings.

Scallops Over Avocado Slices

- 6 ounces fresh *or* frozen scallops
- 1 small avocado, seeded, peeled, and sliced
  Lemon juice
- 2 tablespoons chopped onion
- 1 tablespoon butter *or* margarine
- 1 tablespoon all-purpose flour
- ¼ teaspoon salt
  Dash white pepper
  Dash garlic powder
- ½ cup light cream *or* milk
- 1 slightly beaten egg
- 1 tablespoon dry white wine
- 1 tablespoon snipped parsley

Thaw scallops, if frozen. Cut any large scallops into halves or quarters. Brush avocado slices with lemon juice; set aside.

In a small saucepan cook scallops in enough water to cover for 1 to 2 minutes or till tender; drain.

Meanwhile, in a 1-quart saucepan cook the onion in hot butter or margarine till tender but not brown. Stir in the flour, salt, pepper, and garlic powder. Add the light cream or milk all at once. Cook and stir till mixture is thickened and bubbly. Cook and stir for 1 minute more.

Gradually stir about *half* of the hot mixture into the slightly beaten egg. Return all to saucepan. Stir in the scallops, wine, and snipped parsley; heat through. Spoon the scallop mixture over the avocado slices. Makes 2 servings.

Pictured opposite, from front to back: Scallops Over Avocado Slices and Granola-Stuffed Cornish Hen (see recipe, page 54).

Shrimp-Stuffed Peppers

- ½ cup water
- ¼ cup long grain rice
- ¼ teaspoon salt
- 2 medium green peppers
- 1 7-ounce package frozen shelled shrimp *or* one 4½-ounce can shrimp, drained
- ¼ cup mayonnaise *or* salad dressing
- 1 tablespoon chopped onion
  Dash bottled hot pepper sauce
  Salt
  Pepper
- 3 tablespoons crushed rich round crackers (3 crackers)
- 1 teaspoon butter *or* margarine, melted

In a saucepan combine the water, rice, and salt. Bring to boiling; reduce heat. Cover and cook about 15 minutes; let stand 10 minutes.

Meanwhile, cook the green peppers in boiling salted water for 5 minutes. Cut the tops from the green peppers; remove and discard the seeds, membranes, and tops. Set the cooked green pepper shells aside.

In a saucepan cook the frozen shrimp in boiling salted water for 1 to 3 minutes or till pink; drain. Reserve 2 of the cooked shrimp or the canned shrimp for a garnish, if desired; chop remaining shrimp.

For stuffing, in a mixing bowl combine the cooked rice, chopped shrimp, the mayonnaise, onion, and hot pepper sauce. Season to taste with salt and pepper.

Spoon the stuffing into cooked peppers. Place the stuffed peppers upright in a 7½x3½x2-inch loaf pan. Combine the crushed crackers and butter or margarine; sprinkle atop peppers. Bake, uncovered, in a 350° oven for 40 minutes. Garnish *each* pepper with *one* of the reserved whole shrimp, if desired. Makes 2 servings.

Crispy Shrimp Patties

Serve these golden patties in hamburger buns with tartar sauce and lettuce for tasty shrimp burgers—

- 1 beaten egg
- 3 tablespoons fine dry bread crumbs
- 1 tablespoon green goddess *or* Caesar salad dressing
- 1 4½-ounce can shrimp, drained and chopped
- 2 teaspoons snipped parsley
- 2 tablespoons fine dry bread crumbs
- 1 tablespoon butter *or* margarine
  Tartar sauce (optional)
  Lemon wedges (optional)

In a mixing bowl combine the beaten egg, the 3 tablespoons dry bread crumbs, and the green goddess or Caesar salad dressing. Stir in the shrimp and snipped parsley. Cover and chill the mixture for 30 minutes or till firm.

Shape the chilled shrimp mixture into 2 patties about 3 inches in diameter. Roll the patties in the 2 tablespoons dry bread crumbs to coat evenly.

In an 8-inch skillet melt the butter or margarine. Add the shrimp patties; cook the patties in the hot butter or margarine over medium heat about 2 minutes on each side or till golden brown.

If desired, serve the shrimp patties with tartar sauce and lemon wedges. Makes 2 servings.

Entrées–Eggs & Cheese

Greek Omelet

- ½ of a 10-ounce package frozen chopped spinach
- ¼ cup crumbled feta cheese (1 ounce)
- ¼ cup cream-style cottage cheese, drained
- 2 teaspoons minced dried onion
- ¼ teaspoon dried mint, crushed
  Dash pepper
- 3 or 4 eggs
  Salt
  Pepper
- 1 tablespoon butter or margarine

In a medium saucepan cook spinach according to package directions. Drain well, squeezing out excess liquid. In the same saucepan combine the drained spinach, the feta cheese, cottage cheese, dried onion, mint, and pepper. Heat through over low heat but *do not boil*, stirring occasionally.

Meanwhile, in a mixing bowl beat the eggs with a fork; sprinkle with salt and pepper. In an 8- or 10-inch skillet with flared sides heat the butter or margarine till it sizzles and browns slightly. Lift and tilt the pan to coat the sides. Add the eggs; cook over medium heat. As eggs set, run a spatula around the edge of the skillet, lifting the eggs to allow uncooked portion to flow underneath. When eggs are set but still shiny, remove from heat.

Spoon the spinach mixture onto half of the omelet; fold the other half over mixture. Slide the filled omelet out onto a serving platter. Makes 2 servings.

Egg Cutlets with Mushroom Sauce

- 1 7½-ounce can semi-condensed cream of mushroom soup
- ⅓ cup fine dry bread crumbs
- 1 tablespoon snipped parsley
- ½ teaspoon minced dried onion
- ⅛ teaspoon dry mustard
  Dash pepper
- 4 hard-cooked eggs, chopped
- 1 tablespoon butter or margarine
- 2 tablespoons dry white wine
  Sliced hard-cooked eggs (optional)

In a medium mixing bowl combine *2 tablespoons* of the soup, *2 tablespoons* of the bread crumbs, the snipped parsley, dried onion, dry mustard, and pepper. Add the 4 chopped hard-cooked eggs and mix well. Shape the egg mixture into four patties 4 inches in diameter. Roll the egg patties in the remaining dry bread crumbs to coat evenly.

In a 10-inch skillet cook the patties in hot butter or margarine for 3 to 5 minutes. Turn and cook for 3 to 5 minutes more or till patties are golden brown.

Meanwhile, for sauce, in a small saucepan combine the remaining soup and the wine; cook and stir till heated through.

To serve, spoon the mushroom sauce over the patties. Garnish with the hard-cooked egg slices, if desired. Makes 2 servings.

Crustless Pizza Quiches

You can substitute diced ham or cooked ground sausage for the pepperoni in these two individual quiches—

- 2 eggs
- ¾ cup milk
- 1 tablespoon all-purpose flour
- ¼ teaspoon salt
- ¼ teaspoon dried oregano, crushed
- ¾ cup shredded mozzarella cheese (3 ounces)
- ¼ cup chopped pepperoni
- 2 tablespoons sliced green onion
  Snipped parsley (optional)

In a medium mixing bowl beat the eggs with a fork. Stir in the milk, all-purpose flour, salt, and the dried oregano. Stir the shredded mozzarella cheese, the chopped pepperoni, and the sliced green onion into the egg mixture.

Arrange two 10-ounce custard cups in a shallow baking pan on oven rack. Pour the egg-cheese mixture into the 2 custard cups. Pour boiling water around the custard cups in the baking pan to a depth of 1 inch.

Bake the individual quiches, uncovered, in a 350° oven for 30 to 35 minutes or till a knife inserted near the centers comes out clean. Let the quiches stand for 5 minutes before serving. Sprinkle each of the individual quiches with some snipped parsley, if desired. Makes 2 servings.

Peppery Stuffed Eggplant

1 medium eggplant (about 1 pound)
⅓ cup chopped onion
1 clove garlic, minced
3 tablespoons butter *or* margarine
¾ cup soft bread crumbs (1 slice)
¼ cup chopped walnuts
¼ cup chopped pitted ripe olives
2 tablespoons chopped canned green chili peppers
2 tablespoons lemon juice
1 tablespoon snipped parsley
¼ teaspoon salt
¼ teaspoon dried basil, crushed
1 cup shredded provolone cheese (4 ounces)
4 tomato slices

Halve eggplant lengthwise; scoop out the centers and reserve the pulp, leaving ¼-inch shells (see page 73 for picture). Chop the reserved pulp; set aside.

Cook the eggplant shells, covered, in enough boiling water to cover about 2 minutes or till eggplant is tender. Invert the shells on paper toweling to drain.

For stuffing, in a skillet cook onion and garlic in hot butter or margarine till onion is tender but not brown. Remove from heat. Stir the reserved pulp, the bread crumbs, walnuts, chopped olives, green chili peppers, lemon juice, parsley, salt, and basil into the onion mixture. Stir in *half* of the provolone cheese.

Spoon the stuffing mixture into the eggplant shells (see page 73 for picture). Place the shells upright in a shallow baking pan. Bake, covered, in a 350° oven for 20 minutes. Top *each* stuffed shell with 2 tomato slices. Sprinkle with the remaining provolone cheese. Bake, uncovered, for 5 to 10 minutes more. Makes 2 servings.

Greek-Style Macaroni

1 cup cooked macaroni
1 tomato, chopped
1 teaspoon all-purpose flour
1 tablespoon snipped parsley
¼ teaspoon salt
⅛ teaspoon ground cinnamon
¼ cup finely chopped onion
1 small clove garlic, minced
1 tablespoon butter *or* margarine
2 teaspoons all-purpose flour
½ cup milk
½ cup shredded American cheese (2 ounces)
2 beaten eggs

In a medium mixing bowl combine the cooked macaroni, chopped tomato, the 1 teaspoon flour, the parsley, salt, and cinnamon.

In a small saucepan cook the onion and garlic in hot butter or margarine till tender but not brown. Stir in the 2 teaspoons flour; add the milk all at once. Cook and stir till the mixture is thickened and bubbly; cook and stir for 1 minute more. Reduce heat; stir in the shredded cheese till melted.

Gradually stir the cheese mixture into the beaten eggs; stir into macaroni mixture. Turn the mixture into two 12-ounce au gratin dishes. Bake in a 350° oven for 20 to 25 minutes or till set. Let stand 5 minutes. Makes 2 servings.

Cheesy Beef-Vegetable Boats

2 large onions, green peppers, *or* tomatoes
¼ pound ground beef *or* ground pork
1 small clove garlic, minced
1 beaten egg
¼ cup soft bread crumbs
¼ cup shredded Monterey Jack *or* Swiss cheese (1 ounce)
1 teaspoon vinegar
½ teaspoon Worcestershire sauce
Dash pepper
1 tablespoon grated Parmesan cheese
Curly endive (optional)

If using onions, peel and cook, covered, in boiling water about 25 minutes or till tender; drain. If using peppers, cook the unpeeled peppers, covered, in boiling water for 5 minutes; drain. If using tomatoes, omit this cooking step.

Cut the tops from the vegetables. Scoop out the centers, leaving ¼-inch shells (see page 73 for picture). Reserve the onion or tomato pulp; discard green pepper seeds and membranes. Chop the onion or tomato pulp; set aside. Invert the vegetable shells on paper toweling to drain.

For filling, in a skillet cook the ground beef or pork and garlic till meat is brown. Remove from heat; drain off fat. Stir reserved onion or tomato pulp, egg, bread crumbs, shredded Monterey Jack or Swiss cheese, vinegar, Worcestershire sauce, and pepper into the meat mixture in skillet.

Spoon the filling mixture into the vegetable shells (see page 73 for picture). Sprinkle the grated Parmesan cheese atop stuffed vegetables. Place the filled shells in a shallow baking pan. Bake, uncovered, in a 350° oven about 25 minutes or till heated through. Garnish the vegetables with curly endive, if desired. Makes 2 servings.

Entrées-Salads & Stews

Rancher's Salad Niçoise

Vinaigrette Dressing
1 **small potato**
½ **of a 9-ounce package frozen cut green beans**
2 **cups torn salad greens**
½ **cup cubed cooked beef**
½ **of a medium onion, sliced and separated into rings**
½ **of a small green pepper, sliced into rings**
1 **hard-cooked egg, cut into wedges**
6 **cherry tomatoes *or* 1 medium tomato, cut into wedges**
6 **pitted ripe olives, halved**

Prepare Vinaigrette Dressing. In a covered saucepan cook the potato in boiling salted water about 25 minutes or till tender; drain. Peel and slice potato. Cook the green beans according to the package directions; drain.

Line a salad bowl with the torn salad greens. Arrange the potato slices, green beans, cubed beef, onion rings, green pepper rings, hard-cooked egg wedges, cherry tomatoes or tomato wedges, and olive halves atop greens. Cover and chill for at least 3 hours or overnight.

Before serving, shake the Vinaigrette Dressing; pour *some* of the chilled dressing over the salad. Toss lightly to coat the vegetables. Makes 2 servings.

• **Vinaigrette Dressing:** In screwtop jar combine ½ cup *salad oil*, ⅓ cup *white or red wine vinegar*, 1 teaspoon *sugar*, ½ teaspoon *salt*, and ¼ teaspoon dried *fines herbes*, crushed. Cover the jar tightly and shake to mix the dressing well. Chill for at least 3 hours. Store unused dressing in refrigerator for up to one month.

Ham Salad Strata

1½ **cups torn fresh spinach**
1 **hard-cooked egg, chopped *or* sliced**
4 **slices boiled ham, cut into julienne strips**
½ **of a small red onion, thinly sliced and separated into rings**
½ **cup frozen peas, thawed**
¼ **cup mayonnaise *or* salad dressing**
2 **tablespoons dairy sour cream**
2 **slices bacon**

In a clear salad bowl layer *half* of the spinach, the egg, ham strips, the remaining spinach, the onion rings, and peas. Combine mayonnaise and sour cream; spread over salad, sealing to edge. Cover and chill for up to 24 hours.

Before serving, cook bacon till crisp; drain and crumble. Sprinkle over salad. Makes 2 servings.

Oriental Salad

1 **cup cubed cooked pork**
⅔ **cup cooked rice**
⅓ **cup thinly sliced celery**
¼ **cup fresh bean sprouts**
¼ **cup shredded carrot**
1 **tablespoon sliced green onion**
1 **tablespoon chopped green pepper**
¼ **cup French salad dressing**
1 **tablespoon lemon juice**
2 **teaspoons soy sauce**
2 **tablespoons slivered almonds, toasted**

Combine pork, rice, celery, bean sprouts, carrot, green onion, and green pepper; cover and chill.

In a screw-top jar combine the French dressing, lemon juice, and soy sauce. Cover and shake; chill.

Before serving, shake dressing; pour over salad and toss. Top with almonds. Makes 2 servings.

Barley and Kielbasa Salad

Kielbasa, or Polish sausage, is a beef and pork sausage flavored with garlic and spices—

¼ **cup mayonnaise *or* salad dressing**
¼ **cup plain yogurt**
½ **teaspoon prepared horseradish**
½ **teaspoon Worcestershire sauce**
¾ **cup water**
¼ **teaspoon salt**
¼ **cup quick-cooking barley**
1½ **cups torn fresh spinach *or* romaine**
8 **ounces fully cooked Polish sausage, sliced and quartered**
½ **cup shredded red cabbage**
½ **of a small onion, sliced and separated into rings**

For dressing, in a small mixing bowl combine the mayonnaise or salad dressing, yogurt, horseradish, and the Worcestershire sauce. Cover and chill till serving time.

In a saucepan combine the water and salt; bring to boiling. Stir in the barley; reduce heat. Cover and simmer for 10 to 12 minutes or till barley is tender. Drain the barley and cool.

Before serving, in a salad bowl combine the cooked barley, spinach or romaine, sausage pieces, shredded red cabbage, and onion rings. Pour the dressing over the sausage mixture; toss lightly to coat. Serve the salad immediately. Makes 2 servings.

Chicken Salad with Walnut Dressing

⅓ cup coarsely chopped walnuts
1 tablespoon salad oil
2 tablespoons vinegar
2 tablespoons salad oil
2 teaspoons dry sherry
2 teaspoons soy sauce
¼ teaspoon sugar
⅛ teaspoon salt
1½ cups torn romaine
1 cup cubed cooked chicken
1 small green or red sweet pepper, seeded and cut into 1-inch squares
1 small apple, cored and thinly sliced

For walnut dressing, in a small skillet cook the walnuts in the 1 tablespoon salad oil about 5 minutes or till walnuts are golden brown, stirring occasionally; remove the skillet from heat.

In a screw-top jar combine the undrained browned walnuts, the vinegar, the 2 tablespoons salad oil, the sherry, soy sauce, sugar, and salt. Cover the jar tightly and shake to mix the dressing well. Chill the dressing in the refrigerator for at least 3 hours.

Before serving, in a salad bowl combine the torn romaine, cubed chicken, green or red sweet pepper squares, and the apple slices. Shake the chilled walnut dressing well; pour over the chicken mixture. Toss lightly to coat. Serve immediately. Makes 2 servings.

Beef-Cider Stew

½ pound beef stew meat, cut into 1-inch pieces
1 tablespoon cooking oil
1 5½-ounce can apple cider or apple juice (⅔ cup)
2 teaspoons vinegar
½ teaspoon salt
⅛ teaspoon dried thyme, crushed
⅛ teaspoon pepper
1 medium potato, peeled and cut into eighths
1 medium carrot, sliced ½ inch thick
1 small onion, sliced
1 stalk celery, sliced
3 tablespoons water
4 teaspoons all-purpose flour

In a large saucepan cook the beef stew meat in hot cooking oil till meat is brown on all sides. Drain off fat. Stir in apple cider or apple juice, vinegar, salt, thyme, and pepper. Bring to boiling; reduce heat. Cover and simmer for 1¼ hours or till meat is nearly tender.

Add potato, carrot, onion, and celery. Cook for 30 minutes more or till vegetables are tender. Stir together water and flour; stir into stew. Cook and stir till thickened and bubbly. Cook and stir for 1 minute more. Makes 2 servings.

• **Crockery cooker directions:** In a skillet cook meat in hot cooking oil till brown. Drain off fat. In a mixing bowl combine apple cider or apple juice, vinegar, salt, thyme, and pepper; set aside.

Place potato, carrot, onion, and celery in a 4-cup electric slow crockery cooker. Place the stew meat atop. Pour the apple cider mixture over the meat. Cover and cook the stew on low-heat setting for 10 to 12 hours. Stir together the water and flour; stir into the stew. Cover and cook about 30 minutes more or till thickened.

Bavarian Bratwurst Stew

(pictured on pages 40 and 41)

Serve this robust stew with dark rye or pumpernickel bread—

6 ounces fully cooked smoked bratwurst links, Polish sausage links, beerwurst links, knackwurst links, or frankfurters, cut into thirds
1 8-ounce can sauerkraut, rinsed, drained, and snipped
¾ cup beer
1 small apple, cored and cut into chunks
2 tablespoons finely chopped onion
2 tablespoons raisins
1 tablespoon brown sugar
¼ teaspoon caraway seed
2 tablespoons cold water
4 teaspoons cornstarch

In a 2-quart saucepan combine the bratwurst or other sausage pieces, snipped sauerkraut, beer, apple chunks, chopped onion, raisins, brown sugar, and caraway seed. Bring the sausage mixture to boiling; reduce heat. Cover and simmer for 10 minutes.

Stir together the cold water and the cornstarch. Stir the cornstarch mixture into the sausage mixture in saucepan. Cook and stir till the mixture is thickened and bubbly. Cook and stir for 2 minutes more.

To serve, transfer the stew to a casserole or serving bowl, if desired. Makes 2 servings.

Entrées-Sandwiches

Barbecued Pork Roll-Ups

- **4 ounces ground pork**
- **1 teaspoon minced dried onion**
- **1 tablespoon bottled hot-style barbecue sauce**
- **¼ teaspoon dried basil, crushed**
- **⅛ teaspoon garlic salt**
- **1 stick piecrust mix**
- **¼ teaspoon dried oregano, crushed**
- **½ cup shredded mozzarella cheese**
- **Plain yogurt (optional)**
- **4 pitted ripe olives (optional)**

For filling, in a skillet cook ground pork and dried onion till meat is brown. Drain off fat. Stir in barbecue sauce, basil, and garlic salt.

For dough, in a mixing bowl combine the dry piecrust mix and the oregano; prepare according to package directions. On a lightly floured surface roll dough into an 8x6-inch rectangle.

Spread the filling over dough; sprinkle with the shredded mozzarella cheese. Roll up jelly-roll style, beginning from the longest side (step 1). Moisten the edges of dough with water and seal seam.

Slice the roll into four 2-inch-thick slices (step 2). Place the slices, cut edges down, on a foil-lined baking sheet.

Bake the pork roll-ups in a 375° oven about 25 minutes or till light brown. Before serving, top each with a dollop of yogurt and a ripe olive, if desired. Makes 2 servings.

1 *Spread the pork filling over rectangle of dough and sprinkle it with the shredded cheese. Starting from the longest side, roll the dough up jelly-roll style, as shown.*

Moisten the long edge of the dough with water and press lightly with fingers to seal.

2 *Slice the filled roll of dough into four 2-inch-thick slices. Instead of using a knife (which is likely to squash the rolls), use a strand of ordinary sewing-weight thread.*

Place the thread under the roll of dough where you want to make the cut; pull the thread up around the sides. Criss-cross thread across the top of roll and pull quickly as though tying a knot, as shown. The thread will slice through the dough, making a clean cut.

Slaw-Topped Caraway Burgers

½ cup shredded cabbage
¼ cup finely shredded carrot
1 tablespoon mayonnaise *or* salad dressing
½ teaspoon prepared mustard
 Dash salt
1 beaten egg
1 tablespoon milk
⅓ cup soft bread crumbs
2 tablespoons chopped onion
¼ teaspoon salt
¼ teaspoon dried thyme, crushed
⅛ teaspoon caraway seed
½ pound ground pork *or* ground beef
2 hamburger buns, split and toasted

For topping, in a mixing bowl combine the shredded cabbage, carrot, mayonnaise or salad dressing, mustard, and the dash salt. Set the mixture aside.

For burgers, in a mixing bowl combine the beaten egg and milk; stir in the bread crumbs, onion, the ¼ teaspoon salt, the thyme, and caraway seed. Add ground meat; mix well. Form mixture into two ½-inch-thick patties.

Place the patties on rack of unheated broiler pan. For pork, broil 3 inches from heat for 12 to 15 minutes or till well done. For beef, broil 3 inches from heat to desired doneness, turning once during the cooking period (allow about 8 minutes total time for rare, about 10 minutes for medium, and about 12 minutes for well done).

Place the patties on the bottom halves of buns; top *each* with *half* of cabbage mixture. Top with top halves of buns. Makes 2 servings.

Zucchini Burgers on Rye

1 slightly beaten egg
½ of a small zucchini, shredded (½ cup)
2 tablespoons finely chopped onion
¼ teaspoon salt
⅛ teaspoon pepper
½ pound ground beef
 Green goddess *or* creamy cucumber salad dressing
2 slices rye bread
½ cup alfalfa sprouts *or* shredded lettuce
2 tomato slices

In a medium mixing bowl combine the beaten egg, shredded zucchini, chopped onion, salt, and pepper. Add the ground beef to the zucchini mixture; mix well. Shape the zucchini-meat mixture into two 3/4-inch-thick patties.

Place the zucchini patties on rack of unheated broiler pan. Broil meat 3 to 4 inches from heat to desired doneness, turning patties once during the cooking period (allow about 10 minutes total time for rare, about 12 minutes for medium, and about 18 minutes for well done).

Spread the desired amount of green goddess or creamy cucumber salad dressing on each slice of rye bread. Top each slice with *half* of the alfalfa sprouts or shredded lettuce. Place *one* zucchini burger atop alfalfa sprouts or lettuce on *each* slice of rye bread; top *each* serving with a tomato slice. Makes 2 servings.

Beef and Onion Bagelwiches

¼ cup dairy sour cream
1½ teaspoons prepared horseradish
1½ teaspoons prepared mustard
⅛ teaspoon salt*
 Dash ground red pepper
 Dash paprika
2 unsliced bagels
½ of a small onion, sliced and separated into rings
1 tablespoon butter *or* margarine
5 ounces thinly sliced cooked beef (1 cup) *or* one 3-ounce package thinly sliced smoked beef
 Salt*
 Pepper
 Lettuce leaves

In a small mixing bowl combine sour cream, horseradish, mustard, ⅛ teaspoon salt*, ground red pepper, and paprika.

Slice *each* bagel into thirds horizontally. Place bagel slices on a baking sheet. Broil 4 inches from heat about 3 minutes, turning once to toast both sides.

Meanwhile, in a skillet cook onion rings in hot butter or margarine till almost tender, stirring occasionally. Arrange the sliced beef over onion. Cover and cook over low heat for 5 to 10 minutes or till beef is heated through. Season to taste with salt* and pepper.

To assemble, place the lettuce leaves atop the bottom portions of the bagels. Then layer *half* of the beef, *some* of the sour cream mixture, the center portions of bagels, the remaining beef, onion rings, and some more of the sour cream mixture. Top with the top portions of the bagels. Pass any remaining sour cream mixture with the bagelwiches. Makes 2 servings.

Note: If using sliced smoked beef, omit the salt.

Entrées-Sandwiches

Mandarin-Ham Sandwiches

If you prefer, make this sandwich another time with slices of white or whole wheat bread—

- 2 kaiser rolls
- 1 tablespoon mayonnaise *or* salad dressing
- ¼ teaspoon prepared mustard
- ⅛ teaspoon seasoned salt
- ½ cup finely shredded lettuce
- ¼ cup chopped seeded cucumber
- ¼ cup chopped canned mandarin orange sections
- 1 tablespoon sliced green onion
- 1 6-ounce package thinly sliced boiled ham
  Butter *or* margarine, softened

With a sharp knife slice off the top quarter of each kaiser roll. Remove the soft center from the bottom of *each* roll, leaving a ¼-inch shell. (Reserve centers for another use.)

In a medium mixing bowl combine mayonnaise or salad dressing, prepared mustard, and the salt. Add the shredded lettuce, the chopped cucumber, the chopped mandarin orange sections, and the sliced green onion; toss to coat.

Fill the bottom of *each* roll with *half* of the lettuce mixture; top *each* with *half* of the ham slices.

Spread tops of rolls with softened butter or margarine. Place roll tops, buttered side down, over ham slices. Makes 2 servings.

Salami 'n' Cheese Vegetablewiches

(pictured on pages 40 and 41)

- ½ cup sliced cauliflower flowerets
- ½ cup shredded Monterey Jack cheese (2 ounces)
- 3 ounces salami, cut up
- ¼ cup shredded carrot
- 2 tablespoons chopped dill pickle
- 1 tablespoon sliced green onion
- 2 French-style rolls
- 1 tablespoon butter *or* margarine, softened
- 1 tablespoon mayonnaise *or* salad dressing
- ½ teaspoon prepared mustard
  Leaf lettuce
- 1 small tomato, sliced
- 2 tablespoons Italian salad dressing

If desired, cook cauliflower, covered, in a small amount of boiling salted water for 3 to 5 minutes or till crisp-tender. Drain and chill.

In a mixing bowl combine sliced cauliflower, the shredded Monterey Jack cheese, salami, shredded carrot, chopped pickle, and sliced green onion; toss to mix well.

Cut a ¼-inch slice off the top of each roll. Remove the soft center from the bottom of *each* roll, leaving a ¼-inch shell. (Reserve centers for another use.)

In a mixing bowl combine butter or margarine, mayonnaise or salad dressing, and mustard; spread in bread shells. Line shells with lettuce; spoon the vegetable mixture atop lettuce. Halve tomato slices; place atop filling. Drizzle creamy Italian dressing over all; replace roll tops. Makes 2 servings.

Chicken-Cheese Quesadillas

- ⅔ cup chopped cooked chicken *or* one 5-ounce can chunk-style chicken, cut up
- ½ cup shredded Monterey Jack *or* cheddar cheese (2 ounces)
- 1 canned green chili pepper, rinsed, seeded, and chopped
- ¼ cup taco sauce
- 2 7- *or* 8-inch flour tortillas
- 1 tablespoon butter *or* margarine, melted
  Shredded lettuce
  Shredded Monterey Jack *or* cheddar cheese
  Taco sauce (optional)

In small mixing bowl combine the cooked or chunk-style chicken, the ½ cup shredded Monterey Jack or cheddar cheese, chopped green chili pepper, and the ¼ cup taco sauce.

Spread about *half* of the chicken-cheese mixture onto *each* tortilla. Roll up jelly-roll style.

Place the tortilla roll-ups, seam side down, in a shallow baking dish or a 9-inch pie plate. Brush the roll-ups with the melted butter or margarine. Bake, uncovered, in a 400° oven about 15 minutes or till tortilla roll-ups are heated through.

Sprinkle the warm quesadillas with the shredded lettuce and additional shredded Monterey Jack or cheddar cheese. Pass the additional taco sauce with quesadillas, if desired. Makes 2 servings.

Salmon Egg Rolls

1 8-ounce can salmon, drained, flaked, and bones removed
¼ cup chopped water chestnuts *or* celery
3 tablespoons dairy sour cream *or* mayonnaise
2 tablespoons chopped pickle
1 teaspoon lemon juice
1 teaspoon soy sauce
4 egg roll skins
Cooking oil for deep-fat frying

Combine the salmon, water chestnuts, sour cream or mayonnaise, pickle, lemon juice, and the soy sauce. Place egg roll skins with one point toward you; spoon *some* of the filling just below center of skins. For *each*, fold bottom point over filling; tuck under. Fold in sides, forming an envelope shape. Roll up; seal. Fry egg rolls in ½ inch of hot oil (375°) for 2 to 3 minutes, turning once. Serves 2.

Cheese and Avocado Bagels

1 3-ounce package cream cheese, softened
⅓ cup cream-style cottage cheese with chives
1 teaspoon lemon juice
⅛ teaspoon salt
1 small avocado, seeded, peeled, and chopped
½ cup broken pecans
2 tablespoons chopped pimiento
2 bagels, split and toasted
¼ cup alfalfa sprouts

Beat cheeses, lemon juice, and salt on low speed of electric mixer for 1 minute. Beat for 3 minutes on high. Stir in avocado, nuts, and pimiento; chill. Spread the mixture on bagel halves. Top with sprouts. Makes 2 servings.

Apple-Muenster Rounds

Try this sandwich with Swiss or brick cheese, too—

1 cup shredded muenster cheese (4 ounces)
2 teaspoons milk
1 teaspoon finely chopped green onion
1 teaspoon snipped parsley
1 teaspoon prepared mustard
¼ teaspoon Worcestershire sauce
2 English muffins, split and toasted
1 small apple, cored and sliced
Snipped parsley (optional)

Place the muenster cheese in a small mixer bowl; let stand till the cheese is room temperature. Stir in the milk, chopped green onion, the 1 teaspoon snipped parsley, the prepared mustard, and Worcestershire sauce.

Beat the muenster cheese mixture on medium speed of electric mixer till combined. Spread about *3 tablespoons* of the muenster cheese mixture atop *each* English muffin half.

Place the muffin halves on a baking sheet; broil 4 to 5 inches from heat for 2 to 3 minutes or till cheese starts to melt.

Top *each* muffin half with several apple slices. Broil for 1 to 2 minutes more or till heated through. Garnish with additional parsley, if desired. Makes 2 servings.

Curried Rice Sandwiches

If you're watching your weight, skip the pita bread and serve the rice mixture on the lettuce leaves as a salad—

¾ cup water
⅓ cup brown rice
2 teaspoons instant beef bouillon granules
¾ teaspoon curry powder
2 teaspoons all-purpose flour
½ cup plain yogurt
½ cup peanuts
½ cup chopped apple
¼ cup sliced celery
2 tablespoons toasted wheat germ
1 large pita bread round
Lettuce leaves
1 tablespoon sesame seed, toasted

In a medium saucepan combine the water, brown rice, instant beef bouillon granules, and curry powder. Bring the mixture to boiling; reduce heat. Cover and simmer for 45 to 50 minutes or till the brown rice is tender.

Stir the flour into the yogurt. Stir the yogurt mixture, the peanuts, chopped apple, sliced celery, and toasted wheat germ into the rice mixture. Cook and stir about 5 minutes more or till the mixture is heated through.

To serve, slice the pita bread round in half crosswise to form a pocket. Line the inside of *each* pita bread pocket with lettuce leaves. Spoon *half* of the rice mixture into each bread pocket. Sprinkle the filling with toasted sesame seeds. Makes 2 servings.

Side Dishes–Salads & Soups

Artichoke-Mushroom Salad

Turn this recipe into an easy appetizer for a small party by replacing the sliced mushrooms with mushroom caps and serving the vegetables on wooden picks—

¼ cup salad oil
3 tablespoons lemon juice
1½ teaspoons sugar
1 small clove garlic, minced
¼ teaspoon salt
⅛ teaspoon cracked pepper
⅛ teaspoon dried chervil *or* tarragon, crushed
⅛ teaspoon dried basil, crushed
½ of a 9-ounce package frozen artichoke hearts, cooked and drained
½ cup sliced fresh mushrooms
   Romaine leaves

For marinade, in a screw-top jar combine the salad oil, lemon juice, sugar, minced garlic, salt, pepper, chervil or tarragon, and the basil. Cover the jar tightly and shake to mix the marinade well.

In a mixing bowl combine the cooked artichoke hearts and the mushroom slices. Pour the marinade over the vegetables, tossing to coat. Cover and chill for at least 3 hours or overnight.

Before serving, drain the artichoke heart and mushroom mixture; discard marinade. Arrange the vegetables on individual salad plates lined with romaine leaves. Makes 2 servings.

Dynasty Salad

(pictured on page 68)

1 medium carrot
½ of a medium green pepper, thinly sliced into rings
½ of a 6-ounce package frozen pea pods
1 stalk celery, bias-sliced (½ cup)
½ cup sliced fresh mushrooms
3 tablespoons salad oil
2 tablespoons sake *or* dry sherry
1 teaspoon teriyaki sauce *or* soy sauce
¼ teaspoon ground ginger (optional)
2 teaspoons sesame seed, toasted

With a sharp knife cut five V-shaped ridges lengthwise in the carrot, spacing them evenly. Bias-slice carrot. Cut the green pepper rings in half.

In saucepan cook carrot and green pepper in a small amount of boiling salted water for 4 minutes. Add pea pods; return to boiling. Cook for 1 minute more or till vegetables are crisp-tender; drain.

On 2 individual salad plates, overlap the pea pods around the edges of the plates. Arrange the carrot slices, celery slices, mushroom slices, and green pepper rings in the center. Cover and chill for at least 3 hours.

For dressing, in screw-top jar combine the salad oil, sake or sherry, teriyaki or soy sauce, and ginger, if desired. Cover the jar tightly and shake to mix the dressing well. Chill for at least 3 hours.

Before serving, sprinkle *each* salad with *1 teaspoon* sesame seed. Shake the chilled dressing again and pour over the salad. Makes 2 servings.

Blue Cheese Salad Bowl

For a Greek-style salad, substitute crumbled feta cheese for the blue cheese. Serve either salad with crusty French bread or pita bread rounds—

⅓ cup crumbled blue cheese (1½ ounces)
3 tablespoons salad oil
2 teaspoons lemon juice
⅛ teaspoon sugar
⅛ teaspoon salt
   Dash pepper
   Dash paprika
1 small onion, thinly sliced and separated into rings
¼ cup sliced fresh mushrooms
2 cups torn lettuce *or* romaine
1 medium zucchini, thinly sliced
¼ cup sliced radishes

For marinade, in a screw-top jar combine the blue cheese, salad oil, lemon juice, sugar, salt, pepper, and paprika. Cover the jar tightly and shake to mix the marinade well.

In a mixing bowl combine the onion rings and the sliced fresh mushrooms; pour the marinade over all, tossing lightly to coat. Cover and chill the vegetables for at least 3 hours or overnight.

To serve, in a salad bowl combine the torn lettuce or romaine, sliced zucchini, and sliced radishes. Add the *undrained* onion mixture to the zucchini mixture. Toss the salad lightly to coat the vegetables. Makes 2 servings.

Creamy German Potato Salad

- 2 small potatoes
- 2 slices bacon
- 2 tablespoons chopped onion
- 2 teaspoons sugar
- ½ teaspoon all-purpose flour
- ¼ teaspoon salt
  Dash pepper
- ¼ cup water
- 1 tablespoon vinegar
- ¼ cup dairy sour cream
  Parsley sprigs (optional)

In a medium saucepan cook potatoes in boiling salted water about 25 minutes or till tender. Drain. Peel and slice the warm potatoes.

Meanwhile, in a 10-inch skillet cook the bacon till crisp. Remove and drain on paper toweling, reserving 1 tablespoon drippings in skillet. Crumble bacon; set aside.

Cook the onion in the reserved bacon drippings till tender but not brown. Stir in the sugar, flour, salt, and pepper. Add the water and vinegar all at once. Cook and stir till the mixture is thickened and bubbly. Cook and stir for 1 minute more. Remove from heat.

In a large mixing bowl gradually stir the onion mixture into sour cream. Add the sliced potatoes to the sour cream mixture in bowl. Add *half* of the crumbled bacon; lightly toss the mixture. Return the mixture to skillet. Heat through but *do not boil.*

Turn the warm potato mixture into a serving bowl. Sprinkle the remaining crumbled bacon atop. Garnish with parsley, if desired. Serve warm. Makes 2 servings.

Country Garden Soup

- 1 13¾-ounce can chicken broth
- 1 medium zucchini, sliced ¼ inch thick
- 1 medium carrot, thinly sliced
- 1 stalk celery, bias-sliced
- 1 teaspoon snipped dill *or* ¼ teaspoon dried dillweed
  Dash pepper
- 1 tablespoon dry sherry
- 2 sprigs parsley (optional)

In a saucepan bring chicken broth to boiling. Stir in zucchini, carrot, celery, dill, and pepper. Cover and cook about 10 minutes or till vegetables are crisp-tender. Remove from heat; stir in sherry.

To serve, ladle the soup into 2 soup bowls. Garnish each serving with a sprig of parsley, if desired. Makes 2 servings.

Golden Broccoli Bisque

- 1 cup fresh *or* frozen chopped broccoli
- ¼ cup boiling water
- 1¼ cups milk
- 1 single-serving envelope instant cream of mushroom soup mix
  Dash garlic powder
- ¼ cup shredded cheddar cheese (1 ounce)

In a 1-quart saucepan cook the fresh broccoli in the boiling water for 8 to 10 minutes or till tender. (Or, cook the frozen broccoli in the boiling water for 5 minutes.)

Stir in the milk, mushroom soup mix, and garlic powder. Cook and stir till the mixture is thickened and bubbly.

To serve, ladle the soup into 2 soup bowls. Top *each* serving with *2 tablespoons* of the shredded cheese. Makes 2 servings.

Summer Gazpacho

If you prefer a smooth rather than chunky soup, follow the directions for blending or processing the ingredients—

- 1 6-ounce can vegetable juice cocktail
- ⅓ cup beef broth
- ¼ cup chopped green pepper
- 1 small tomato, peeled and chopped
- ¼ cup chopped onion
- 1 small clove garlic, minced
- 2 tablespoons lemon juice
- 1 teaspoon olive *or* cooking oil
- 1 teaspoon paprika
  Dash pepper
  Seasoned croutons, sliced green onion, chopped peeled avocado, chopped tomato, *or* chopped cucumber

In a large mixing bowl combine the vegetable juice cocktail, the beef broth, chopped green pepper, the 1 chopped tomato, the chopped onion, minced garlic, lemon juice, olive or cooking oil, paprika, and pepper. (Or, place ingredients in blender container or food processor bowl. Cover; blend or process for 30 seconds or till of desired consistency.) Cover and chill in refrigerator for at least 3 hours or overnight.

To serve, ladle the chilled soup into soup bowls and garnish with the seasoned croutons, the sliced green onion, the chopped avocado, the additional chopped tomato, or the chopped cucumber. Makes 2 servings.

Cashew-Mushroom Soup

1 tablespoon butter *or* margarine
2 teaspoons all-purpose flour
Dash ground nutmeg
Dash pepper
½ cup chicken broth
½ cup light cream *or* milk
½ cup sliced fresh mushrooms
¼ cup coarsely chopped cashews
Sliced fresh mushrooms

In a 1-quart saucepan melt the butter or margarine. Stir in the flour, nutmeg, and the pepper. Add the chicken broth and light cream or milk all at once. Cook and stir over medium heat till the mixture is thickened and bubbly. Cook and stir for 1 minute more. Stir in the ½ cup sliced mushrooms and the cashews; heat through.

Carefully pour the mushroom mixture into blender container or food processor bowl. Cover and blend or process till the mixture is nearly smooth.

Return the blended mixture to saucepan; heat through. Season to taste with salt and pepper. To serve, ladle the soup into 2 soup bowls; garnish each serving with the additional sliced fresh mushrooms. Makes 2 servings.

Hot Egg Drop Soup

1 13¾-ounce can chicken broth
1 stalk celery with leaves, chopped
1 tablespoon sliced green onion
Dash bottled hot pepper sauce
Dash ground ginger
1 well-beaten egg

In a saucepan combine the chicken broth, the chopped celery with leaves, green onion, bottled hot pepper sauce, and the ground ginger. Bring mixture to boiling.

Slowly pour the beaten egg into the soup; stir once gently so the egg forms thin shreds. Remove from heat. Serve the soup immediately. To serve, ladle the soup into 2 soup bowls. Makes 2 servings.

Onion-Cheese Soup

⅓ cup chopped onion
1 tablespoon butter *or* margarine
4 teaspoons all-purpose flour
⅛ teaspoon salt
Dash pepper
1½ cups milk
¾ cup shredded American cheese (3 ounces)
Paprika
Snipped chives

In a 1-quart saucepan cook the onion in hot butter or margarine till tender but not brown. Stir in flour, salt, and pepper. Add milk all at once. Cook and stir till thickened and bubbly. Cook and stir for 1 minute more. Remove from heat.

Add the shredded cheese to the hot mixture; stir till melted. Ladle the soup into 2 soup bowls. Garnish each serving with paprika and snipped chives. Makes 2 servings.

Easy Tortilla Soup

Prepare this Mexican-style soup when you want to use leftover corn tortillas—

4 corn tortillas
Cooking oil for deep-fat frying
1 medium tomato, peeled and cored
½ of a small onion, cut up
1 small clove garlic
⅛ teaspoon crushed red pepper
1 tablespoon cooking oil *or* olive oil
2 cups chicken broth
⅓ cup shredded cheddar cheese

Cut the tortillas into ¼-inch strips. In a skillet heat ½ inch of cooking oil to 375°. Fry the tortilla strips, a few at a time, in hot oil for 45 to 60 seconds or till strips are crisp and light brown. Drain the tortilla strips on paper toweling. Set aside.

In a blender container or food processor bowl combine peeled tomato, onion, garlic, and crushed red pepper; cover and blend or process till chopped.

In a 1-quart saucepan combine the chopped tomato mixture and the 1 tablespoon cooking oil or olive oil. Cook, uncovered, for 10 minutes. Add the chicken broth. Bring to boiling; reduce heat. Cover and simmer the mixture for 10 minutes more.

Stir the fried tortilla strips and the shredded cheese into the tomato-broth mixture; serve immediately. To serve, ladle the soup into 2 soup bowls. Makes 2 servings.

Pictured opposite from front to back: Dynasty Salad (see recipe, page 66) and Hot Egg Drop Soup.

Side Dishes–Vegetables

Creamy Chilled Green Beans

- 2 tablespoons dairy sour cream
- 2 tablespoons Italian salad dressing
- 1 8-ounce can cut green beans, drained
- 1 tomato, peeled, chopped, and drained
- 2 tablespoons finely chopped onion
- 2 lettuce cups

In a mixing bowl stir together the sour cream and the Italian salad dressing. Stir the drained beans, chopped tomato, and chopped onion into the sour cream mixture. Cover and chill for at least 3 hours.

To serve, spoon the bean mixture into lettuce cups. Makes 2 servings.

Deviled Green Beans

- 1 8-ounce can cut green beans
- 1½ teaspoons butter or margarine
- ½ teaspoon Dijon-style mustard
- ½ teaspoon Worcestershire sauce

In a saucepan heat the *undrained* beans; drain. Turn the beans into a serving bowl; keep warm.

In the same saucepan melt the butter or margarine. Stir in the mustard and the Worcestershire sauce. Pour the mustard mixture over the hot beans; toss lightly to coat the beans. Makes 2 servings.

Carrot and Olive Stir-Fry

- 2 medium carrots, bias-sliced ¼ inch thick
- 2 tablespoons sliced green onion
- ⅛ teaspoon dried dillweed *or* basil, crushed
  Dash pepper
- 1 tablespoon olive oil *or* cooking oil
- 2 tablespoons sliced pitted ripe olives

In a saucepan cook the carrot slices in boiling salted water about 10 minutes or just till tender; drain.

In an 8-inch skillet cook the green onion, dillweed or basil, and pepper in hot olive oil or cooking oil for 1 minute. Add the carrots; cook and stir over medium heat for 8 to 10 minutes or till light brown. Stir in the sliced ripe olives and heat through. Makes 2 servings.

Pea Pod Stir-Fry

- 1 tablespoon soy sauce
- 1 teaspoon cornstarch
- ⅓ cup water
- 1 tablespoon dry sherry
- ½ teaspoon sugar
- 1 tablespoon cooking oil
- 1 6-ounce package frozen pea pods, thawed
- ¼ cup walnut halves

In a bowl combine soy sauce and cornstarch; stir in the water, sherry, and sugar. Set aside.

Preheat a wok or skillet over high heat; add oil. Stir-fry pea pods in hot oil for 1 minute or till crisp-tender. (Add more oil, if necessary.) Add walnut halves; stir-fry for 1 minute. Stir soy mixture; stir into wok. Cook and stir till thickened and bubbly. Cover and cook 2 minutes more. Makes 2 servings.

Caraway Cheese Green Beans

- 8 ounces fresh green beans, cut into pieces (1½ cups), *or* one 9-ounce package frozen cut green beans
- ⅓ cup milk
- 1 tablespoon all-purpose flour
- 1 tablespoon finely chopped onion
- ⅛ teaspoon salt
  Dash pepper
- 1 ounce caraway cheddar cheese, crumbled (¼ cup)
- 2 tablespoons dairy sour cream

In a medium saucepan cook the fresh green beans, covered, in a small amount of boiling salted water about 15 minutes or till tender. (*Or*, cook the frozen green beans according to package directions.) Drain. Transfer the beans to a serving bowl and keep warm.

In a small saucepan stir together the milk and flour. Stir the chopped onion, salt, and pepper into saucepan. Cook and stir over low heat till the mixture is thickened and bubbly. Cook and stir for 1 minute more. Remove the thickened mixture from heat.

Add crumbled caraway cheddar cheese; stir till melted. Stir in the sour cream; return to heat and heat through but *do not boil*.

Pour the caraway cheese mixture over the hot, drained green beans. Toss lightly to coat. Makes 2 servings.

Swiss Cheese-Spinach Cups

½ of a 10-ounce package frozen chopped spinach
1 tablespoon butter *or* margarine
½ cup shredded Swiss cheese (2 ounces)
½ cup chopped water chestnuts
1 slightly beaten egg
3 tablespoons milk
1 tablespoon chopped onion
1 tablespoon chopped pimiento
⅛ teaspoon ground nutmeg
Ground nutmeg (optional)

In a saucepan cook the chopped spinach according to package directions. Drain well, squeezing out excess liquid. Stir in the butter or margarine till melted. Stir in *half* of the Swiss cheese, the chopped water chestnuts, beaten egg, milk, chopped onion, pimiento, and the ⅛ teaspoon ground nutmeg.

Place 2 well-greased 10-ounce custard cups in a baking pan. Turn the spinach-egg mixture into the custard cups. Pour boiling water into pan around the custard cups to a depth of 1 inch. Bake in a 350° oven about 35 minutes or till a knife inserted near the centers comes out clean.

Sprinkle the tops of the spinach custards with the remaining shredded Swiss cheese. Bake the spinach cups for 2 to 3 minutes more. Sprinkle each serving with the additional ground nutmeg, if desired. Makes 2 servings.

Zucchini Mexicali

½ cup thinly sliced zucchini (6 ounces)
1 small carrot, coarsely shredded
⅓ cup chopped onion
¼ cup chopped celery
¼ of a medium green pepper, cut into thin strips
2 tablespoons cooking oil
¼ teaspoon garlic salt
⅛ teaspoon dried basil, crushed
Dash pepper
3 tablespoons taco sauce
1 teaspoon prepared mustard
1 medium tomato, cut into wedges
Salt

In an 8-inch skillet or wok combine the sliced zucchini, shredded carrot, chopped onion, chopped celery, green pepper strips, cooking oil, garlic salt, basil, and pepper. Toss to coat the vegetables evenly.

Cover and cook the vegetables over medium heat for 4 minutes or till carrot is crisp-tender, stirring occasionally.

In a small mixing bowl combine the taco sauce and mustard; stir into the vegetable mixture in the skillet or wok. Add the tomato wedges to the vegetable mixture. Cook, uncovered, for 3 to 5 minutes more or till the mixture is heated through. Season to taste with salt. Serve from the skillet or wok or transfer to a serving dish. Makes 2 servings.

Cooking Vegetables

When you cook vegetables, protect the nutrients you purchased.

Prepare just the right amount for the two of you to eat in one meal. Reheating the leftovers can cause loss of vitamin C.

When cooking vegetables, use as little liquid as possible to retain water-soluble B and C vitamins. Prolonged cooking will also destroy nutrients.

Cook any frozen vegetables from their frozen state. Thawing them in advance allows vitamin loss.

Turnip in Cheese Sauce

1 large turnip, peeled and quartered
1 tablespoon butter *or* margarine
2 teaspoons all-purpose flour
¼ teaspoon salt
Dash pepper
⅓ cup milk
¼ cup shredded American cheese (1 ounce)
Snipped parsley
Paprika

Cook turnip in boiling salted water for 12 to 15 minutes. Drain.

Melt butter. Stir in flour, salt, and pepper. Add milk; cook and stir till thickened and bubbly. Cook and stir for 1 minute more. Remove from heat; stir in cheese till melted. Stir in turnip pieces; heat through. Garnish with parsley and paprika. Makes 2 servings.

Side Dishes–Vegetables

Potato-Apple Skillet

2 small potatoes, peeled and cut into ¼-inch julienne strips
1 medium apple, cored and chopped (1 cup)
1 small stalk celery, bias-sliced
¼ cup chopped onion
1 tablespoon cooking oil
Dash salt
Dash pepper
⅓ cup shredded cheddar cheese (1½ ounces)

In a medium skillet combine the potato strips, apple, celery, onion, cooking oil, salt, and pepper.

Cover and cook over low heat for 15 to 20 minutes or till the vegetables are tender, stirring occasionally. Sprinkle the cheese over potato mixture. Makes 2 servings.

Hashed Brown Potatoes

2 small baking potatoes or 2 medium red potatoes
1 tablespoon finely chopped onion
¼ teaspoon salt
Dash pepper
2 tablespoons butter or margarine

In a covered saucepan cook the unpeeled potatoes in boiling salted water for 25 to 30 minutes or just till tender. Drain and chill.

Peel chilled potatoes; coarsely shred to measure 1½ cups. Add the chopped onion, salt, and dash pepper to the shredded potato.

Melt butter in an 8-inch skillet. Pat potato mixture into skillet, leaving ½-inch space around edge. Cook, uncovered, over medium heat about 6 minutes or till underside is crisp. Turn potato; reduce heat. Cook about 5 minutes more or till crisp. Makes 2 servings.

Sweet Potato Casserole

The coconut topping toasts as the casserole bakes—

1 medium sweet potato *or* 2 small sweet potatoes (12 ounces) *or* one 8-ounce can sweet potatoes, drained
1 tablespoon butter *or* margarine, melted
1 tablespoon raisins
½ teaspoon finely shredded orange peel
⅛ teaspoon ground cinnamon
Dash ground nutmeg
2 tablespoons flaked coconut
1 teaspoon butter *or* margarine, melted

Scrub the fresh sweet potatoes with a brush. In a saucepan cook fresh sweet potatoes in enough boiling salted water to cover for 30 to 40 minutes or till tender; drain and peel.

Mash the cooked, fresh sweet potatoes or canned sweet potatoes. Stir the 1 tablespoon melted butter or margarine, raisins, orange peel, cinnamon, and nutmeg into the mashed potatoes. Turn the sweet potato mixture into an ungreased 10-ounce custard cup.

For topping, toss the coconut with the 1 teaspoon melted butter or margarine. Sprinkle the coconut mixture atop the sweet potato mixture in custard cup. Bake, uncovered, in a 350° oven for 20 to 25 minutes or till casserole is heated through. Makes 2 servings.

Sweet Potato-Bacon Boats

2 medium sweet potatoes
3 slices bacon *or* 3 tablespoons cooked bacon pieces
¼ cup shredded cheddar cheese (1 ounce)
1 tablespoon butter *or* margarine, softened
Dash salt
Dash pepper
Shredded cheddar cheese (optional)

Scrub the sweet potatoes with a brush. Place in a shallow baking pan. Bake in a 350° oven about 1 hour or till tender.

Meanwhile, in a skillet cook the bacon slices till crisp. Remove and drain on paper toweling. Crumble the bacon and set aside. (*Or,* use cooked bacon pieces.)

Cut a lengthwise slice from the top of *each* sweet potato; discard the skins from top slices. Scoop out the centers, being careful not to break shells. Set the shells aside. Combine the sweet potato centers with portions from top slices; mash slightly with a fork.

For filling, in a mixer bowl combine the mashed sweet potato, the ¼ cup cheddar cheese, the butter or margarine, salt, and pepper. Beat on high speed of electric mixer till fluffy. Fold in *2 tablespoons* of the crumbled bacon or cooked bacon pieces. Spoon the sweet potato mixture into the reserved potato shells.

Return filled potato shells to the shallow baking pan. Bake in a 350° oven about 10 minutes or till heated through. Top with additional shredded cheddar cheese, if desired and the remaining crumbled bacon or cooked bacon pieces. Makes 2 servings.

Spinach-Stuffed Tomatoes

- **2 medium tomatoes**
- **2 slices bacon**
- **2 tablespoons chopped onion**
- **4 ounces fresh spinach, snipped**
- **¼ cup dairy sour cream**
- **1½ teaspoons all-purpose flour**
- **⅛ teaspoon salt**
- **Dash bottled hot pepper sauce**
- **¼ cup shredded mozzarella cheese (1 ounce)**

Cut the tops from the tomatoes (step 1). Discard tops. Scoop out the centers, leaving tomato shells (step 2). Discard the tomato pulp. Invert the vegetable shells on paper toweling to drain. Sprinkle the shells with salt.

In a skillet cook bacon till crisp. Remove and drain on paper toweling, reserving 1 tablespoon of the drippings in the skillet. Crumble the bacon and set aside.

For filling, cook the chopped onion in reserved drippings till tender; stir in the spinach. Cover and cook for 3 to 5 minutes or till tender. Remove from heat. Stir together the sour cream, flour, salt, and bottled hot pepper sauce; stir into the spinach mixture. Stir in the bacon pieces.

Spoon the spinach filling into the drained tomato shells (step 3). Place the filled shells in a shallow baking pan. Bake in a 375° oven about 15 minutes or till heated through. Top with shredded mozzarella cheese; bake for 2 to 3 minutes more or till cheese is melted. Makes 2 servings.

1 *With a sharp paring knife, carefully slice off the top portion of each tomato, as shown. Be sure to cut enough off to allow a teaspoon to fit inside the tomato. Discard the top slices.*

2 *Using a teaspoon, scoop out tomato centers, leaving the tomato shells, as shown.*

Remove as much liquid from the inside of the tomato shell as possible to prevent the filling from becoming too wet. Discard tomato pulp. Drain the tomato shells, upside down, on paper toweling while preparing filling.

3 *Using a teaspoon, spoon the spinach filling into the drained, salted tomato shells, as shown. Pack the filling loosely to prevent the shells from breaking. Place the filled tomato shells in a shallow baking pan and bake as directed.*

Side Dishes–Rice & Pasta

Broccoli Risotto

For a true risotto, rice must be prepared using a unique method that originated in Northern Italy. The rice is first cooked in hot fat, then simmered in a seasoned broth till it is still slightly firm but the mixture is creamy—

- ⅓ cup long grain rice
- 2 tablespoons chopped onion
- 1 clove garlic, minced
- 1 tablespoon olive oil *or* cooking oil
- ¾ cup water
- ½ cup fresh *or* frozen cut broccoli
- 1 teaspoon instant chicken boullion granules
- ¼ teaspoon Italian seasoning
  Dash pepper
- 2 tablespoons grated Parmesan cheese

In a medium saucepan cook the uncooked rice, chopped onion, and garlic in hot olive oil or cooking oil about 4 minutes or till the rice is golden brown and the onion is tender but not brown. Stir in the water, fresh or frozen broccoli, chicken bouillon granules, Italian seasoning, and pepper.

Bring the rice mixture to boiling; reduce heat. Cover and simmer for 15 minutes (do not lift cover). Remove from heat. Stir the Parmesan cheese into the rice mixture. Cover and let stand for 5 to 8 minutes or just till rice is tender but slightly firm and the mixture is creamy. Makes 2 servings.

Brown Rice Puff

- ⅓ cup quick-cooking brown rice
- 2 tablespoons sliced green onion
- 1 tablespoon butter *or* margarine
- 1½ teaspoons all-purpose flour
- ¼ teaspoon fines herbes
- ½ cup milk
- 1 egg yolk
- 2 tablespoons grated Parmesan cheese
- 1 egg white

In a small saucepan cook the quick-cooking brown rice according to package directions.

Meanwhile, in a small saucepan cook the green onion in hot butter or margarine till tender but not brown. Stir in the flour and fines herbes. Add the milk all at once. Cook and stir till the mixture is thickened and bubbly. Cook and stir for 1 minute more. Remove from heat.

In a small mixer bowl beat the egg yolk on high speed of electric mixer till thick and lemon colored. Gradually add the thickened milk mixture to the egg yolk, stirring constantly. Stir the cooked brown rice and the Parmesan cheese into the yolk mixture.

Using clean beaters, in a mixer bowl beat the egg white till stiff peaks form (tips stand straight). Gradually fold the rice mixture into the beaten egg white.

Turn the mixture into an ungreased 2- or 3-cup soufflé dish. Bake in a 350° oven about 30 minutes or till a knife inserted near the center comes out clean. Serve immediately. Makes 2 servings.

Walnut-Bulgur Pilaf

- ½ cup water
- ¾ teaspoon instant beef bouillon granules
- ¼ cup bulgur wheat
- ½ teaspoon finely shredded orange peel (optional)
- 2 tablespoons orange juice
- ½ teaspoon cornstarch
- 1 tablespoon cooking oil
- ½ of a medium red *or* green sweet pepper, chopped
- 2 tablespoons chopped walnuts *or* pine nuts

In a saucepan combine the water and beef bouillon granules; cook and stir till bouillon granules are dissolved. Remove from heat. Stir the bulgur into the bouillon and let the mixture stand for 1 hour. Drain the mixture, pressing out any excess liquid. Set bulgur aside.

In a small mixing bowl stir together the orange peel, if desired; the orange juice; and the cornstarch. Set aside.

Preheat a wok or medium skillet over high heat. Add the cooking oil. Stir-fry the red or green sweet pepper and walnuts or pine nuts for 2 minutes or till the pepper is crisp-tender and the walnuts or pine nuts are golden brown.

Stir the orange juice mixture; stir into the wok. Cook and stir till the mixture is thickened and bubbly. Add the drained bulgur and toss lightly; cover and cook about 1 minute more or till heated through. Makes 2 servings.

Fettuccine with Spinach Pesto

Serve leftover pesto with meats, fish, vegetables, or soups—

- 1 **cup torn fresh spinach**
- ⅓ **cup grated Parmesan cheese**
- ¼ **cup chopped walnuts**
- 1 **small clove garlic**
- ¾ **teaspoon dried basil**
- ¼ **teaspoon salt**
- **Dash pepper**
- 3 **tablespoons olive oil** *or* **cooking oil**
- 3 **ounces fettuccine** *or* **spaghetti**
- 2 **tablespoons sliced pimiento**

For pesto, in a blender container or food processor bowl combine the spinach, Parmesan cheese, walnuts, garlic, dried basil, salt, and pepper. Cover and blend or process with several on/off turns till a paste forms. With machine running slowly, gradually add the olive oil or cooking oil. Blend or process to the consistency of soft butter, stopping and pushing the mixture into the blade as necessary.

Remove the pesto from the container. Divide the pesto into 3 portions; set one portion aside. Wrap and freeze the remaining 2 portions for later use.*

Cook the fettuccine or spaghetti according to package directions; drain. Stir the reserved portion of pesto into the cooked pasta. Add the sliced pimiento and toss lightly to coat. Serve warm or chilled. Makes 2 servings.

*Note: Thaw the frozen pesto in the refrigerator before using.

Pasta and Prosciutto

- 6 **ounces fresh mushrooms, halved (2 cups)**
- 3 **ounces prosciutto** *or* **sliced fully cooked ham, cut into 1-inch strips (½ cup)**
- ¼ **cup chopped onion**
- 2 **tablespoons butter** *or* **margarine**
- ¼ **cup light cream** *or* **milk**
- ½ **teaspoon dried basil, crushed**
- **Dash pepper**
- ¼ **cup dry white wine** *or* **chicken broth**
- 3 **ounces spaghetti, linguine,** *or* **other pasta**
- 2 **tablespoons butter** *or* **margarine**
- ¼ **cup grated Parmesan cheese**
- 2 **tablespoons snipped parsley**
- **Grated Parmesan cheese (optional)**

In a skillet cook the mushroom halves, prosciutto or ham, and chopped onion in 2 tablespoons hot butter or margarine till vegetables are tender. Stir in the cream or milk, basil, and pepper. Bring to boiling; add wine or broth. Cook over medium heat for 12 minutes or till the mixture is slightly thickened, stirring occasionally.

Meanwhile, cook the pasta according to the package directions; drain. Transfer the pasta to a warm serving dish.

Toss the pasta with 2 tablespoons butter or margarine. Stir in the ¼ cup Parmesan cheese, and the parsley. Pour the mushroom mixture over pasta; toss lightly to coat. Serve immediately. Pass additional Parmesan cheese, if desired. Makes 2 servings.

Zucchini-Lasagna Rolls

- 2 **lasagna noodles**
- 1 **medium zucchini, chopped**
- 1 **7½-ounce can tomatoes, cut up**
- 2 **tablespoons chopped green olives**
- 1 **tablespoon chili sauce**
- ¼ **teaspoon Italian seasoning**
- ½ **cup ricotta** *or* **cream-style cottage cheese, drained**
- 2 **tablespoons grated Parmesan cheese**
- **Grated Parmesan cheese**

Cook lasagna noodles according to package directions. Drain and set aside. Meanwhile, in a covered saucepan cook zucchini in a small amount of boiling water about 5 minutes or till tender. Drain the zucchini and set aside.

Meanwhile, for sauce, in a small saucepan combine the *undrained* tomatoes, the green olives, chili sauce, and Italian seasoning. Bring to boiling; reduce heat. Simmer, uncovered, for 7 to 8 minutes or till the mixture is slightly thickened.

For filling, in a mixing bowl stir together the zucchini, *¼ cup* of the sauce, ricotta or cottage cheese, and the 2 tablespoons Parmesan cheese.

Spread *each* lasagna noodle with *half* of the zucchini filling. Roll up jelly-roll style, beginning at narrow end. Place the rolls, seam side down, in a greased 8x8x2-inch baking dish. Spoon the remaining sauce over rolls. Sprinkle with additional Parmesan cheese. Cover and bake the rolls in a 375° oven about 25 minutes or till heated through. Makes 2 servings.

Side Dishes–Breads

Bran-Prune Coffee Bread

- 1 tablespoon all-purpose flour *or* 1 tablespoon toasted wheat germ
- 1 tablespoon brown sugar
- ¼ teaspoon ground cinnamon
- 1 tablespoon butter *or* margarine
- ½ cup all-purpose flour
- 1 teaspoon baking powder
- ¼ teaspoon salt
- 1 beaten egg
- ½ cup milk
- ¼ cup sugar
- 1 tablespoon cooking oil
- ¼ teaspoon vanilla
- ⅓ cup bran flakes
- ¼ cup chopped pitted dried prunes

Lightly grease a 20-ounce casserole; set aside.

For topping, in a small mixing bowl combine the 1 tablespoon flour or wheat germ, the brown sugar, and cinnamon. Cut in the butter or margarine till the mixture resembles fine crumbs; set aside.

In a large mixing bowl stir together the ½ cup flour, the baking powder, and the salt. In a small mixing bowl combine the beaten egg, the milk, sugar, cooking oil, and vanilla. Add the milk mixture to the dry ingredients, stirring just till moistened. Stir in the bran flakes and the chopped prunes. Pour the batter into the prepared casserole.

Sprinkle the cinnamon topping atop batter. Bake in a 350° oven about 35 minutes or till a wooden pick inserted near center comes out clean. Cool in the casserole for 10 minutes. Remove the bread from the casserole and cool on a wire rack. Makes 1.

Dill Quick Bread

Serve one loaf of this dill-flavored quick bread with soup, fish, or poultry. If you like, wrap, label, and freeze the second loaf for later—

- 1 cup all-purpose flour
- ¼ cup whole wheat flour
- 2 tablespoons sugar
- 1½ teaspoons baking powder
- 1 teaspoon dillseed
- ¼ teaspoon salt
- 1 beaten egg
- ⅔ cup milk
- 3 tablespoons butter *or* margarine, melted

Grease two 4½x2½x1½-inch individual loaf pans; set aside.

In a medium mixing bowl stir together the all-purpose flour, the whole wheat flour, sugar, baking powder, dillseed, and salt. In a small mixing bowl combine the beaten egg, milk, and the melted butter or margarine.

Add the milk mixture all at once to the dry ingredients in the medium mixing bowl. With a fork stir the mixture just till the dough is moistened. Turn the dough into the prepared loaf pans.

Bake the loaves in a 350° oven for 35 to 40 minutes or till a wooden pick inserted near the centers of the loaves comes out clean. Remove the bread from the loaf pans. Cool the loaves on a wire rack.

If desired, to store, wrap *one* of the loaves in moisture-vaporproof wrap; seal, label, and freeze for up to 2 months. Makes 2 loaves.

Banana Coffee Ring

- 2 tablespoons brown sugar
- 2 tablespoons butter *or* margarine
- 4 maraschino cherries, halved
- 2 tablespoons coconut
- ½ cup all-purpose flour
- ¾ teaspoon baking powder
- ⅛ teaspoon baking soda
- ⅛ teaspoon salt
- ⅓ cup sugar
- 2 tablespoons butter *or* margarine
- 1 egg
- ½ teaspoon vanilla
- ⅓ cup mashed banana
- 3 tablespoons buttermilk *or* sour milk

For topping, in a small saucepan combine the brown sugar and 2 tablespoons butter or margarine. Cook and stir just till the butter or margarine is melted. Pour into the bottom of a 3-cup ring mold. Arrange the cherry halves in the brown sugar-butter mixture; sprinkle coconut atop. Set aside.

In a medium mixing bowl stir together the flour, baking powder, baking soda, and salt. In a large mixer bowl combine the sugar and 2 tablespoons butter or margarine; beat on high speed of electric mixer till well combined. Add the egg and vanilla; beat well.

Add the flour mixture, mashed banana, and buttermilk or sour milk alternately to the butter mixture, beating till smooth after each addition. Spoon the batter over coconut and cherries in ring mold.

Bake in a 350° oven for 30 to 35 minutes or till done. Immediately turn out onto a platter or wire rack. Serve warm or cool. Makes 1.

Pictured opposite from front to back: Cheddar-Apple Bread (see recipe, page 79), Banana Coffee Ring, and Lemon Yogurt Muffins (see recipe, page 78).

Side Dishes–Breads

Serving Muffins

To warm any leftover muffins, wrap them in foil and heat them in a 400° oven for 15 to 20 minutes. (Or, reheat one unwrapped muffin in a counter-top microwave oven on high power for 15 to 20 seconds or 4 muffins for 25 to 30 seconds.)

Lemon Yogurt Muffins

(pictured on page 77)

⅔ cup all-purpose flour
2 tablespoons toasted wheat germ
1 tablespoon sugar
1 teaspoon baking powder
¼ teaspoon salt
2 tablespoons shortening
1 beaten egg
½ cup lemon yogurt
½ teaspoon finely shredded lemon peel

Line a muffin pan with 6 paper bake cups; set aside.

In a medium mixing bowl stir together the flour, wheat germ, sugar, baking powder, and salt. Cut in shortening till the mixture resembles coarse crumbs. Make a well in the center of the mixture.

In another mixing bowl combine the beaten egg, yogurt, and peel; add all at once to dry ingredients. Stir just till ingredients are moistened (the batter should be lumpy).

Fill the prepared muffin cups ⅔ full. Bake in a 375° oven for 20 to 25 minutes. Remove from pan. Serve warm. Makes 6 muffins.

Oatmeal-Raisin Muffins

You'll love the spicy flavor and the crisp crust of these wholesome muffins—

½ cup all-purpose flour
2 tablespoons sugar
1 teaspoon baking powder
¼ teaspoon salt
⅛ teaspoon ground allspice
⅓ cup quick-cooking rolled oats
1 beaten egg
⅓ cup milk
¼ cup cooking oil
2 tablespoons honey
⅓ cup raisins*

Grease a muffin pan or line with 6 paper bake cups; set aside.

In a medium mixing bowl stir together the flour, the sugar, baking powder, salt, and allspice. Stir in the rolled oats; make a well in the center of the mixture.

In a small mixing bowl combine the beaten egg, milk, cooking oil, and honey. Add the egg mixture all at once to the center of the dry ingredients. Stir just till the dry ingredients are moistened (the batter should be lumpy). Fold the raisins into the batter.

Fill the prepared muffin cups ⅔ full with batter. Bake the muffins in a 400° oven for 15 to 20 minutes or till golden. Remove the muffins from the pan. Serve warm. Makes 6 muffins.

*Note: Plump the raisins, if you desire. In a small mixing bowl pour boiling water over the raisins to cover. Let stand for 5 minutes. Drain the raisins.

Pimiento-Mushroom Fritters

These golden puffs can be served as a snack or appetizer, or with a meal—

½ cup all-purpose flour
1 teaspoon baking powder
⅛ teaspoon salt
¼ cup milk
2 tablespoons chopped fresh mushrooms
1 tablespoon chopped pimiento
1 teaspoon sliced green onion
Shortening *or* cooking oil for deep-fat frying

In a medium mixing bowl stir together the all-purpose flour, the baking powder, and the salt. Make a well in the center of the flour mixture.

Add the milk all at once to the flour mixture. With a fork stir the mixture just till the dry ingredients are moistened (the batter should be lumpy). Stir the chopped fresh mushrooms, the chopped pimiento, and the sliced green onion into the fritter batter.

In a heavy medium saucepan or deep-fat fryer heat 1½ inches of shortening or cooking oil to 375°. Drop the fritter batter by rounded tablespoonfuls into the hot shortening or cooking oil.

Fry the fritters, a few at a time, about 1½ minutes on each side or till golden brown. Remove the fritters from pan and drain on paper toweling. Serve warm. Makes 8 or 9 fritters.

Cheddar-Apple Bread

(pictured on page 77)

- **1 to 1¼ cups all-purpose flour**
- **¾ cup whole wheat flour**
- **1 package active dry yeast**
- **½ cup apple cider *or* apple juice**
- **1 small apple, peeled and shredded (½ cup)**
- **1 tablespoon butter *or* margarine**
- **½ teaspoon salt**
- **¼ cup finely shredded cheddar cheese**

In a mixer bowl combine ¾ *cup* of the all-purpose flour, the whole wheat flour, and the yeast.

In a small saucepan heat the apple cider or juice, apple, butter or margarine, and salt just till warm (115° to 120°) and butter is almost melted, stirring constantly.

Add the warm liquid to the flour mixture. Beat on low speed of electric mixer for ½ minute, scraping sides of bowl constantly. Beat 3 minutes on high speed. Stir in the cheese. Stir in as much of the remaining all-purpose flour as you can mix in with a spoon.

Turn mixture out onto a lightly floured surface. Knead in enough of the remaining all-purpose flour to make a moderately stiff dough that is smooth and elastic (6 to 8 minutes total). Shape into a ball. Place in a lightly greased bowl; turn once to grease the surface. Cover and let rise in a warm place till double (45 to 60 minutes).

Punch the dough down; cover and let rest 10 minutes. Lightly grease a 7½x3½x2-inch loaf pan. Shape the dough into a loaf. (*Or,* to braid the dough, see tip, above right). Place the dough in the prepared loaf pan. Cover and let the dough rise in a warm place till nearly double (about 30 minutes). Bake in a 375° oven for 25 to 30 minutes or till done, covering with foil, if necessary. Makes 1 loaf.

Farina Corn Bread

Farina is a meal or flour made from wheat that is often marketed as a hot breakfast cereal—

- **¾ cup all-purpose flour**
- **½ cup white *or* yellow cornmeal**
- **½ cup quick-cooking farina**
- **1 tablespoon sugar**
- **2 teaspoons baking powder**
- **½ teaspoon baking soda**
- **½ teaspoon salt**
- **1 beaten egg**
- **⅔ cup milk**
- **3 tablespoons cooking oil**

Grease two 6x3x2-inch loaf pans; set aside. In a medium mixing bowl stir together the flour, white or yellow cornmeal, farina, sugar, baking powder, baking soda, and salt. Make a well in the center of the mixture.

In another mixing bowl combine the beaten egg, milk, and cooking oil. Add the milk mixture all at once to the cornmeal mixture. With a fork stir the cornmeal mixture just till the batter is smooth; do not overbeat.

Turn the cornmeal batter into the 2 prepared loaf pans. Bake the loaves in a 375° oven for 25 to 30 minutes or till a wooden pick inserted near the centers comes out clean. Cool the corn bread slightly in the loaf pans. Remove loaves from the pans. Cool on a wire rack. If desired, wrap *one* of the loaves in moisture-vaporproof wrap; seal, label, and freeze for later use. Makes 2 loaves.

Braiding Bread

Prepare dough and let rise once as directed in recipe.

Punch the dough down and divide it into thirds; shape each third into a ball. Cover; let rest 10 minutes. On lightly floured surface roll each ball into a thick rope 12 inches long. Line up the three ropes 1 inch apart.

Beginning in the middle of ropes and working toward the ends, braid the ropes loosely and gently straighten. Pinch the ends together and tuck under. Arrange in loaf pan; bake as directed.

Herbed Cheese Crescents

- **1 package (4) refrigerated crescent rolls**
- **¼ cup shredded cheddar cheese (1 ounce)**
- **⅛ teaspoon dried oregano, crushed**
- **⅛ teaspoon celery seed**
- **Dash onion powder**
- **Dash garlic powder**

Unroll refrigerated crescent rolls and separate into 4 triangles. Top *each* triangle with ¼ of the shredded cheddar cheese. In a small mixing bowl combine the oregano, celery seed, onion powder, and garlic powder. Sprinkle the seasoning mixture atop the cheese.

Roll up triangles, beginning at wide edge and rolling toward the point. Place rolls, point side down, on a greased baking sheet. Curve the ends of each to form crescent shapes. Bake in a 375° oven for 10 to 12 minutes or till golden. Serve warm. Makes 4 crescents.

Desserts

Yogurt Puff Baskets

- 2 **tablespoons butter** *or* **margarine**
- ¼ **cup boiling water**
- ¼ **cup all-purpose flour**
  Dash salt
- 1 **egg**
- 1 **8-ounce carton fruit yogurt**
- ⅓ **cup frozen whipped dessert topping, thawed**
  Fresh fruit*

In a small saucepan melt the butter or margarine in the boiling water. Add the flour and salt all at once; stir vigorously by hand. Cook and stir over medium heat till the flour mixture forms a ball that doesn't separate. Remove from heat; cool slightly, about 5 minutes.

Add the egg, beating vigorously with a wooden spoon for 1 minute or till smooth (step 1).

Drop the batter onto a greased baking sheet in two portions at least 3 inches apart. Bake in a 400° oven for 30 to 35 minutes or till golden brown and puffy.

With a sharp knife, split the puffs in half horizontally (step 2). Remove any soft dough inside. Cool the puffs thoroughly on a wire rack.

Cut a ¾-inch-thick strip from *each* cream puff top to form a "basket handle" (step 3); set the strip aside.

For filling, place the yogurt in a small mixing bowl. Fold the thawed dessert topping into yogurt. Spoon the yogurt filling into cream puff bottoms. Arrange whole or sliced fresh fruit atop filling. Place a basket handle atop *each* puff (step 4). Makes 2 servings.

***Note:** Choose from the following fresh fruit: raspberries, blueberries, banana slices, peach slices, strawberry slices, apple slices, or pineapple chunks.

1 *Add the egg to the slightly cooled mixture; beat vigorously with a wooden spoon. At first, the mixture will separate into clumps, as shown. Continue beating with the spoon till the mixture is thick, smooth, and slightly sticky to the touch.*

2 *A delicate pastry, cream puffs are raised by steam and may collapse when they are removed from the oven. You can prevent this by splitting each puff immediately after baking.*

To split cream puffs, cut them in half horizontally with a sharp knife using a sawing motion, as shown.

3 *Cut a ¾-inch-thick strip from each cream puff top to form a "basket handle," as shown.*

Reserve the remaining cream puff top pieces for another use; serve with ice cream or pudding.

4 *After spooning the yogurt filling into cream puff bottoms and arranging fresh fruit atop filling, place a "basket handle" over each filled cream puff, as shown.*

Sour Cream-Apple Puff

(pictured on pages 40 and 41)

- 1 tablespoon butter *or* margarine
- 1 large cooking apple, peeled, cored, and sliced (1 cup)
- 2 tablespoons sugar
- ½ teaspoon finely shredded lemon peel (set aside)
- 1 teaspoon lemon juice
- 2 beaten egg yolks
- ¼ cup dairy sour cream
- ½ teaspoon vanilla
- 2 egg whites
- 2 tablespoons sugar
  Powdered sugar (optional)

In a 6- or 8-inch oven-going skillet melt the butter or margarine. Add the apple slices, 2 tablespoons sugar, and the lemon juice. Cook, uncovered, for 8 to 10 minutes or till the liquid is almost absorbed. Remove *half* of the apple slices; set aside.

In a small mixing bowl stir together the beaten egg yolks, sour cream, vanilla, and lemon peel.

In a small mixer bowl beat the egg whites on high speed of electric mixer till soft peaks form (tips curl over). Gradually add 2 tablespoons sugar to egg whites, beating till stiff peaks form (tips stand straight). Fold the egg yolk mixture into the beaten egg whites.

Pour the mixture over the apples in the skillet. Arrange the reserved apple slices atop. Bake in a 350° oven for 18 to 20 minutes or till golden brown and puffed. Sprinkle powdered sugar atop the baked puff, if desired. Serve immediately. Makes 2 servings.

Aniseed Cakes

You can bake these in a regular muffin pan, too—

- ½ cup all-purpose flour
- ½ teaspoon aniseed, crushed
- ¼ teaspoon baking powder
- ⅛ teaspoon salt
- 3 tablespoons butter *or* margarine
- ½ cup sugar
- 1½ teaspoons finely shredded orange peel
- 1 egg
- 3 tablespoons dairy sour cream
- 3 tablespoons orange juice
- 2 tablespoons sugar

Lightly grease and flour a 2¾-inch fluted muffin pan.

In a small mixing bowl stir together the flour, aniseed, baking powder, and salt; set aside.

In a small mixer bowl beat the butter or margarine on medium speed for 30 seconds. Add the ½ cup sugar and the orange peel and beat till well combined. Add the egg; beat with mixer on medium speed for 1 minute.

Add the flour mixture and sour cream alternately to the creamed mixture, beating on low speed after each addition.

Fill the prepared muffin pan ⅔ full with the batter. Bake in a 375° oven for 15 to 18 minutes or till a wooden pick inserted in the centers comes out clean. Invert the pan onto a wire rack over a tray. Cool the cakes slightly in the pan.

Meanwhile, for glaze, in a small saucepan stir together the orange juice and the 2 tablespoons sugar; bring to boiling; reduce heat.

Remove the cakes from muffin pan; return cakes to the wire rack (over tray). Pierce holes in the fluted tops of cakes with the tines of a fork. Spoon the glaze very slowly over cakes. Cool glazed cakes thoroughly. Store any extra cakes in a tightly covered container for up to 1 week. Makes 8 cakes.

Coconut Macaroon Cupcakes

- ½ cup all-purpose flour
- ⅛ teaspoon salt
- ¼ cup butter *or* margarine
- ⅓ cup sugar
  Few drops almond extract
- 1 egg
- ⅓ cup coconut, toasted
  Powdered sugar (optional)

Grease and lightly flour a muffin pan or line the pan with 6 paper bake cups.

In a small mixing bowl stir together the flour and salt; set the mixture aside.

In a small mixer bowl beat the butter or margarine on medium speed of electric mixer for 30 seconds. Add the sugar and almond extract and beat till the mixture is fluffy. Add the egg; beat the mixture on medium speed of electric mixer for 1 minute.

Add the flour mixture to the beaten mixture and beat on low speed of electric mixer till combined. Stir the toasted coconut into the beaten mixture.

Fill the prepared muffin cups ⅔ full with batter. Bake the cupcakes in a 375° oven for 20 to 25 minutes or till a wooden pick inserted in the centers comes out clean.

Remove the cupcakes from the muffin pan and cool on a wire rack. Sprinkle some powdered sugar atop the cooled cupcakes, if desired. Makes 6 cupcakes.

Desserts

Honey Snaps

1¼ **cups all-purpose flour**
¼   **teaspoon salt**
¼   **teaspoon ground cinnamon**
¼   **teaspoon ground ginger**
⅛   **teaspoon ground cloves**
⅓   **cup butter *or* margarine**
⅓   **cup packed brown sugar**
2   **tablespoons honey**

In a small mixing bowl stir together the flour, salt, cinnamon, ginger, and cloves; set aside.

In a small mixer bowl beat the butter or margarine on medium speed of electric mixer for 30 seconds. Add brown sugar and beat till fluffy. Add honey; beat well. Add the flour mixture to the butter mixture and beat till well combined. Cover and chill for 45 minutes.

Shape dough into two 3-inch-long rolls. Wrap each roll in waxed paper or plastic wrap. Chill at least 6 hours or overnight.

Remove dough from refrigerator and reshape. Unwrap and cut into slices about ⅛ inch thick. Place the slices 1 inch apart on an ungreased cookie sheet. Bake in a 375° oven about 10 minutes or till light brown. Remove and cool on a wire rack. Makes 36 cookies.

Almond Sugar Cookies

¾   **cup all-purpose flour**
¼   **teaspoon baking powder**
⅛   **teaspoon salt**
⅓   **cup butter *or* margarine**
⅓   **cup sugar**
1   **tablespoon milk**
¼   **teaspoon vanilla**
    Few drops almond extract

In a small mixing bowl stir together the flour, baking powder, and salt; set aside.

In a small mixer bowl beat the butter or margarine on medium speed of electric mixer for 30 seconds. Add the sugar and beat till fluffy. Add the milk, vanilla, and almond extract; beat well.

Add the flour mixture to the butter mixture and beat till well combined. Cover and chill the dough for 45 minutes for easier handling, if desired.

Shape the dough into a 4-inch-long roll. Wrap the roll of cookie dough in waxed paper or clear plastic wrap. Chill in the refrigerator for at least 6 hours or till dough is firm enough to cut.

Remove the dough from the refrigerator and reshape slightly to round out the flattened side. Unwrap and cut the dough into slices about ⅛ inch thick. Place the slices of dough about 1 inch apart on an ungreased cookie sheet. Bake in a 375° oven for 8 to 10 minutes or till cookies are light brown. Remove and cool cookies on a wire rack. Makes about 24 cookies.

Chocolate-Mint Rounds

1   **cup all-purpose flour**
2   **tablespoons finely crushed hard peppermint candies**
2   **tablespoons unsweetened cocoa powder**
¼   **teaspoon baking powder**
¼   **teaspoon salt**
¼   **cup butter *or* margarine**
½   **cup sugar**
1   **egg**
½   **teaspoon vanilla**

In a small mixing bowl stir together the flour, peppermint candies, cocoa powder, baking powder, and salt; set aside.

In a small mixer bowl beat the butter or margarine on medium speed of electric mixer for 30 seconds. Add the sugar and beat till fluffy. Add egg and vanilla; beat well.

Add the flour mixture to the butter mixture and beat till well combined. Cover and chill the dough for 45 minutes for easier handling, if desired.

Shape the dough into a 5-inch-long roll. Wrap the roll in waxed paper or clear plastic wrap. Chill in the refrigerator for at least 6 hours or overnight.

Remove the dough from the refrigerator and reshape slightly to round out the flattened side. Unwrap and cut the dough into slices about ¼ inch thick. Place the slices of dough about 1 inch apart on a greased cookie sheet. Bake in a 375° oven for 8 to 10 minutes or till done. Remove and cool the cookies on a wire rack. Makes about 24 cookies.

Blueberry Cobbler

- 1 cup fresh, frozen, *or* canned blueberries
- 2 tablespoons sugar
- ¼ cup all-purpose flour
- ⅛ teaspoon baking powder
- 1 egg yolk
- 1 tablespoon sugar
- 1 tablespoon cooking oil
- 1 tablespoon water
- ½ teaspoon vanilla
- 1 egg white
  Lemon yogurt *or* dairy sour cream (optional)

Clean fresh blueberries. *(Or,* thaw frozen berries. Drain thawed or canned berries.) Combine blueberries and the 2 tablespoons sugar. Turn the berry mixture into a 16-ounce shallow baking dish; set aside.

In a small mixing bowl stir together the flour and baking powder; set aside.

In a small mixer bowl beat the egg yolk, the 1 tablespoon sugar, the cooking oil, water, and vanilla on high speed of electric mixer or with rotary beater about 5 minutes or till thick and lemon colored.

Add the flour mixture to the egg yolk mixture; beat just till the batter is smooth.

Using clean beaters, beat the egg white till stiff peaks form (tips stand straight). Gently fold beaten egg white into the batter. Pour the mixture over blueberries.

Bake in a 350° oven for 25 to 30 minutes or till done. Serve warm. Dollop each serving with lemon yogurt or sour cream, if desired. Makes 2 servings.

Banana-Pecan Fold-Overs

- ⅔ cup all-purpose flour
- ¼ teaspoon salt
- 3 tablespoons shortening *or* lard
- 1 to 2 tablespoons cold water
- 1 medium banana, sliced
- 1½ teaspoons lemon juice
- 2 tablespoons chopped pecans
- 1 tablespoon brown sugar
- ⅛ teaspoon ground cinnamon
  Milk
  Sugar
  Pressurized dessert topping *or* frozen whipped dessert topping, thawed (optional)

For pastry, in a small mixing bowl stir together the flour and salt. Cut in the shortening or lard till pieces are the size of small peas. Sprinkle *1 tablespoon* of the water over part of the mixture; gently toss with a fork. Push to side of bowl. Repeat till all is moistened. Form dough into a ball. On a lightly floured surface roll and trim the dough into a 12x6-inch rectangle. Cut the rectangle in half, forming two 6-inch squares.

Place several banana slices in the center of *each* pastry square; sprinkle with the lemon juice. Top *each* with *1 tablespoon* of the pecans. Combine the brown sugar and cinnamon; sprinkle over *each* square.

For *each* fold-over, fold one side of dough over filling diagonally; moisten edges with water and seal with the tines of a fork.

Place the foldovers on an ungreased baking sheet. Brush with milk and sprinkle with sugar. Bake in a 425° oven for 15 to 17 minutes or till golden brown. Serve warm. Top with dessert topping, if desired. Makes 2 servings.

Plum-Filled Pastries

- 1 cup all-purpose flour
- 1 tablespoon sugar
- ½ teaspoon salt
- ¼ cup shortening
- 3 tablespoons butter *or* margarine
- 1 to 2 tablespoons cold water
- ⅓ cup chopped pitted canned purple plums, drained
- 2 tablespoons chopped walnuts
- ¼ cup sugar
  Milk
  Powdered sugar *or* cinnamon sugar

For pastry, in a small mixing bowl stir together the flour, the 1 tablespoon sugar, and the salt. Cut in the shortening and butter or margarine till pieces are the size of small peas. Sprinkle *1 tablespoon* of the water over part of the mixture; gently toss with a fork. Push to side of bowl. Repeat till all is moistened. Form the dough into 2 balls. On a lightly floured surface roll each *half* to ⅛-inch thickness. Cut each *half* into 12 rounds with a 2½-inch cookie cutter.

Cover *half* of the dough rounds with the chopped plums and walnuts; sprinkle with the ¼ cup sugar. Top with the remaining dough rounds; moisten edges with water and seal with the tines of a fork.

Place the filled pastries on an ungreased cookie sheet. Make a small cut in the tops and brush with milk. Bake in a 425° oven for 12 to 15 minutes or till golden brown. Remove and cool on a wire rack. Sprinkle powdered sugar or cinnamon sugar atop pastries. Makes 12 pastries.

Desserts

Trifle Cake Cups

The rich vanilla sauce and sherry-soaked cake are reminiscent of an English trifle—

½ cup fresh, frozen, *or* canned berries*
1 5-ounce can vanilla pudding
2 tablespoons milk
½ teaspoon vanilla
2 cake dessert cups
2 tablespoons cream sherry
  Pressurized dessert topping *or* frozen whipped dessert topping, thawed (optional)
  Sliced almonds, toasted (optional)

Clean the fresh berries. (*Or,* thaw the frozen berries. Rinse and drain the thawed or canned berries.) Slice any large berries; set aside.

For vanilla sauce, in a small mixing bowl combine the canned vanilla pudding, milk, and vanilla.

Place the cake dessert cups on 2 individual dessert plates. Sprinkle *each* cake cup with *1 table-spoon* of the cream sherry. Spoon *half* of the berries onto *each* cup. Spoon *half* of the vanilla sauce over *each* filled cup.

Garnish each serving with the whipped dessert topping and the sliced almonds, if desired. Makes 2 servings.
*Note: Choose from the following fresh, frozen, or canned berries: blueberries, blackberries, straw-berries, and red raspberries.

Poached Pears in Red Wine

2 small pears, peeled
½ cup water
1 teaspoon lemon juice
⅔ cup dry *or* sweet red wine
2 tablespoons sugar
2 inches stick cinnamon

Core pears, working from bottom and leaving stem intact. In a small mixing bowl combine the water and lemon juice. Place the pears in the lemon juice mixture.

In a small saucepan combine the wine, sugar, and stick cinnamon; bring to boiling. Cover and cook for 5 minutes. Drain pears; add to wine mixture. Cover and simmer for 10 to 15 minutes or till pears are tender, turning pears once.

Transfer the pears to 2 individual dessert dishes. Continue cooking syrup, uncovered, till reduced to ¼ cup. Remove the stick cinnamon. Pour the syrup over pears; cover and chill. Makes 2 servings.
• **Microwave directions:** Use ingredients as above, *except* use only ½ cup red wine.

Prepare the pears as directed above and place in the lemon juice mixture in a 1-quart nonmetal casserole.

In a 2-cup glass measure combine the wine, sugar, and the stick cinnamon. Cook, uncovered, in a counter-top microwave oven on high power for 2 minutes, stirring after 1 minute.

Drain the pears; add the hot wine mixture to pears in the casserole. Cover and micro-cook on high power about 7 minutes or till the pears are tender, rotating dish a quarter-turn every 2 minutes. Remove the stick cinnamon.

Transfer the pears to 2 individual dessert dishes. Pour the red wine syrup over pears. Cover and chill till serving time.

Fruit and Rice Parfaits

½ cup milk
⅓ cup quick-cooking rice
1 teaspoon cream sherry (optional)
¼ teaspoon vanilla
1 cup fresh *or* frozen unsweetened fruit*
  Sugar (optional)
½ cup frozen whipped dessert topping, thawed
1 tablespoon sliced almonds, toasted

In a small saucepan combine the milk and rice. Bring to boiling; reduce heat. Cover and cook about 5 minutes or till liquid is absorbed. Stir in the cream sherry, if desired, and the vanilla. Cool slightly; cover and chill mixture.

Clean fresh fruit. (*Or,* thaw and drain frozen fruit.) Slice or cut up any large pieces. If desired, reserve 2 pieces of fruit for a garnish. Sprinkle sugar on remaining fruit, if desired; set aside.

Fold the thawed dessert topping into the chilled rice mixture. To assemble the parfaits, in 2 parfait glasses layer *some* of the fruit, *some* of the almonds, *some* of the rice mixture, and *some* more of the almonds. Repeat the layers twice, ending with the almonds on top. Garnish *each* parfait with *one* of the reserved pieces of fruit, if desired. Cover and chill till serving time. Makes 2 servings
*Note: Choose from the following fresh or frozen fruit: strawberries, blueberries, blackberries, red raspberries, or peach slices.

Pictured opposite from front to back: Trifle Cake Cups, Poached Pears in Red Wine, and Fruit and Rice Parfaits.

Desserts

To grate chocolate, grate a solid square of chocolate with a hand grater, blender, or food processor.

When shaving chocolate, use a vegetable peeler to shave pieces from a firm square of chocolate.

For chocolate curls, let one bar of sweet chocolate come to room temperature, then carefully draw peeler across wide, flat side.

Keep some chocolate-flavored sprinkles, chocolate-flavored syrup, and cocoa powder on hand for quick chocolate garnishes.

Fruit Kabobs

- 2 tablespoons honey
- 1 teaspoon orange juice
  Dash ground cloves
- 1 medium apple, cored, quartered, and cut into chunks
- 1 medium banana, cut into 1-inch chunks
- 4 maraschino cherries
- ¼ cup grated coconut *or* ground peanuts
- ⅓ cup orange yogurt

In a small mixing bowl combine honey, orange juice, and cloves.

On 4 wooden skewers alternately thread the apple chunks, banana chunks, and the cherries; brush with the honey mixture.

Broil kabobs 4 inches from heat for 3 to 5 minutes or till heated through, turning once. *(Or,* grill over *medium* coals for 5 minutes, turning often.) Sprinkle with coconut or peanuts after turning. Serve with the yogurt. Makes 2 servings.

Black Forest Cream

- ½ of an 8¾-ounce can pitted light sweet cherries *or* 12 pitted fresh dark sweet cherries
- 1 square (1 ounce) semisweet chocolate
- ⅔ cup vanilla ice cream
- ⅓ cup frozen whipped dessert topping, thawed
- 1 tablespoon cherry brandy *or* brandy

Lightly oil two 6-ounce molds or custard cups; set aside. Drain the canned cherries (reserve the remaining canned cherries for another use). Chop the canned cherries or fresh cherries and set aside.

If desired, for garnish shave 4 thin curls from chocolate with vegetable peeler. (*Or,* see tip, above left for another garnish.) Cover and chill chocolate curls till serving time. Chop the remaining chocolate and set aside.

In a chilled mixing bowl stir ice cream just to soften. Gently stir the thawed dessert topping and cherry brandy or brandy into the softened ice cream. Fold in the chopped cherries and chopped chocolate. Pour the mixture into prepared molds or custard cups. Cover and freeze for 3 hours or till firm.

Before serving, let stand 10 minutes. If desired, unmold the frozen cream onto 2 dessert dishes. Garnish each serving with the chocolate curls or another chocolate garnish. Makes 2 servings.

Butterscotch-Rum Custards

- ⅔ cup light cream *or* milk
- 3 tablespoons butterscotch pieces
- 1 tablespoon sugar
  Dash salt
- 1 slightly beaten egg
- 1 teaspoon rum *or* ¼ teaspoon rum flavoring
- 2 tablespoons chopped walnuts *or* pecans
  Pressurized dessert topping (optional)

Lightly grease two 6-ounce custard cups; set aside. In a heavy saucepan combine the light cream or milk, butterscotch pieces, sugar, and salt. Cook and stir over low heat till the butterscotch pieces are melted; cool slightly. Gradually stir about *half* of the butterscotch mixture into the egg; return all to pan. Stir in the rum or rum flavoring.

Place prepared custard cups in a shallow baking pan on oven rack. Divide the custard mixture between the cups. Pour boiling water into pan around cups to depth of 1 inch. Sprinkle *1 tablespoon* of the walnuts or pecans atop *each* custard.

Bake the custards in a 350° oven about 30 minutes or till a knife inserted near the centers comes out clean. Serve warm or chilled.

To unmold the chilled custards, loosen edges with a knife; invert onto plates. Garnish with the topping, if desired. Makes 2 servings.

• **Peanut Butter Custards:** Prepare Butterscotch-Rum Custards as above, *except* substitute 3 tablespoons *peanut butter-flavored pieces* for the butterscotch pieces and omit the nuts and the rum or rum flavoring.

Individual Lime Cheesecakes

- 1 3-ounce package cream cheese, softened
- ½ teaspoon finely shredded lime peel (optional)
- 1 tablespoon lime juice
- 1 *or* 2 drops green food coloring (optional)
- 1 egg white
- 2 tablespoons sugar
- 2 graham cracker tart shells
  Pressurized dessert topping *or* frozen whipped dessert topping, thawed (optional)
- 2 lime twists (optional)

In a mixer bowl combine the cream cheese, lime peel if desired, lime juice, and food coloring if desired. Beat on medium speed of electric mixer till fluffy; set aside.

In a small mixer bowl beat the egg white on high speed of electric mixer till soft peaks form (tips curl over). Gradually add the sugar, beating till stiff peaks form (tips stand straight). Fold the beaten egg white into the cream cheese mixture.

Spoon the cream cheese mixture into the graham cracker tart shells. Bake in a 350° oven for 10 minutes. (Cakes will puff, then fall when removed from oven.) Cool slightly. Cover the cheesecakes loosely with clear plastic wrap or waxed paper and chill in the refrigerator at least 3 hours.

Garnish each serving with dessert topping and a lime twist, if desired. Makes 2 servings.

Watermelon Slush

- 1 tablespoon sugar
- 1 tablespoon orange liqueur
- 1 tablespoon lemon juice
- 1 cup seeded and cubed watermelon *or* cantaloupe

In a blender container combine the sugar, orange liqueur, and lemon juice; add watermelon or cantaloupe. Cover and blend till smooth. Pour the blended mixture into a 7½x3½x2-inch loaf pan. Cover and freeze at least 4 hours.

To make slush, scrape a spoon across the surface of the frozen mixture. Spoon the slush into dessert glasses. Makes 2 servings.

Marmalade Bread Pudding

- 1 beaten egg
- ¼ cup milk
- 1 tablespoon sugar
  Dash ground cloves
- ¾ cup soft bread crumbs (1 slice)
- 2 tablespoons orange marmalade

Lightly grease two 6-ounce custard cups; set aside. In a small mixing bowl stir together the beaten egg, milk, sugar, and cloves.

Place the bread crumbs in the prepared custard cups. Pour the egg mixture over bread crumbs. Cover with foil and bake in a 325° oven for 25 minutes.

Place *1 tablespoon* of the marmalade atop *each* bread pudding. Bake for 5 to 10 minutes more or till a knife inserted near the centers comes out clean. Serve warm. Makes 2 servings.

Peanut Butter-Oatmeal Crunch Topper

You can layer this tasty topper with some ice cream, frozen yogurt, pudding, or chopped fruit to make jiffy parfaits—

- 2 tablespoons butter *or* margarine
- 2 tablespoons brown sugar
- 2 tablespoons chunk-style peanut butter
- 2 teaspoons light corn syrup
- 1 cup quick-cooking rolled oats

In a small saucepan melt the butter or margarine; stir in the brown sugar, peanut butter, and corn syrup. Cook and stir over low heat till combined. Remove from heat.

Add the rolled oats to the peanut butter mixture, stirring till oats are well coated. Spread the mixture evenly in an ungreased shallow baking pan. Bake in a 350° oven for 12 to 15 minutes or till the mixture is golden brown, stirring once or twice to prevent overbrowning the edges. Cool completely without stirring. Crumble with fingers to break up any large pieces.

To serve, spoon the topper over ice cream, frozen yogurt, pudding, or chopped fruit.

Store the unused portion in a covered container in the refrigerator up to 2 weeks. (*Or,* store unused topper in clear plastic bags; seal, label, and freeze.) Makes about 1½ cups topper.

Desserts

Basic Dessert Crêpes

- 1 **beaten egg**
- ¾ **cup milk**
- ½ **cup all-purpose flour**
- 1 **tablespoon sugar**
- 1½ **teaspoons cooking oil**
  Dash salt

In a mixing bowl combine the egg, milk, flour, sugar, cooking oil, and salt. Beat till smooth.

Heat a lightly greased 6-inch skillet. Remove from heat. Spoon in *2 tablespoons* of the batter; lift and tilt skillet to spread batter. Return to heat; brown on one side only. Invert pan over paper toweling; remove crêpe. Repeat with the remaining batter, greasing skillet occasionally.

To store unused crêpes, stack the crêpes alternately with sheets of waxed paper. Place in a moisture-vaporproof bag. Seal, label, and freeze. Makes 10 crêpes.

Mocha Crêpes

- 1 **5-ounce can chocolate pudding**
- 2 **tablespoons chopped pecans**
- ½ **teaspoon instant coffee crystals**
- ½ **teaspoon vanilla**
- 4 **Basic Dessert Crêpes (see recipe above)**

For filling, in a small mixing bowl combine pudding, pecans, coffee crystals, and vanilla.

For packet fold, spoon ¼ of the filling in center of unbrowned side of a Basic Dessert Crêpe. Fold 2 opposite edges to overlap atop filling. Fold remaining edges toward center to form a square packet (step 1). Repeat with remaining.

Place crêpes, seam side down, in a 6x6x2-inch baking dish. Cover and bake in a 350° oven about 12 minutes or till heated through. If desired, garnish with chocolate (see tip, page 86). Makes 2 servings.

1 *To fold the crêpe in a packet fold, spoon some of the filling in the center of the unbrowned side of the crêpe. Fold one of the edges over the filling. Fold the opposite edge over, enclosing the filling. Fold one open end over the center; fold the remaining end over the center, as shown, forming a square packet.*

2 *To roll a crêpe jelly-roll-style, spread some of the filling over the surface of the unbrowned side of the crêpe. Starting at one edge, roll up the crêpe with the filling to the inside, as shown.*

3 *To fold the crêpe in a lapped fold, spoon some of the filling in a line down the center of the unbrowned side of the crêpe. Fold one of the crêpe edges over the filling. Fold opposite edge over, as shown, enclosing the filling.*

4 *To fold the crêpe in a quarter fold, spoon some of the filling in the center of unbrowned side. Fold the crêpe in half with the browned side to the outside, forming a semicircle. Fold crêpe in half again, forming a triangle.*

Rather than filling the crêpes, cook the unfilled crêpes in a sauce in a skillet, as shown.

Pineapple-Coconut Crêpes

- 1 **8-ounce can crushed pineapple (juice pack)**
- 1 **3-ounce package cream cheese, softened**
- 2 **tablespoons coconut**
- 4 **Basic Dessert Crêpes (see recipe opposite)**
- ¾ **teaspoon cornstarch Toasted coconut (optional)**

Drain pineapple, reserving juice. For filling, in a small mixing bowl stir together pineapple, cheese, and the 2 tablespoons coconut.

To assemble in a jelly-roll fold, spread about ¼ of the filling over unbrowned side of a Basic Dessert Crêpe; roll up (step 2). Repeat with remaining filling and crêpes.

Place the filled crêpes, seam side down, in a greased 8x6½x2-inch baking dish. Cover and bake in a 350° oven about 12 minutes or till heated through.

Meanwhile, for sauce, in saucepan combine reserved pineapple juice and the cornstarch. Cook and stir till thickened and bubbly. Cook and stir for 2 minutes more.

To serve, spoon the pineapple sauce atop crêpes. Garnish each serving with the toasted coconut, if desired. Makes 2 servings.

Spicy Banana Shake

- 1 **medium banana**
- 1 **cup milk**
- ⅛ **teaspoon ground cinnamon Dash ground cloves Dash ground nutmeg**

Cut banana into 1-inch pieces. Wrap pieces in foil and freeze.

Unwrap the banana pieces. In a blender container combine the banana pieces, the milk, cinnamon, cloves, and nutmeg. Cover; blend till smooth. Makes 2 servings.

Almond Cream Crêpes

- 2 **tablespoons sugar**
- 1 **teaspoon all-purpose flour**
- ¼ **cup milk**
- 1 **slightly beaten egg**
- 2 **tablespoons ground almonds**
- 1 **teaspoon butter *or* margarine**
- ½ **teaspoon vanilla Few drops almond extract**
- 4 **Basic Dessert Crêpes (see recipe opposite) Sliced almonds, toasted (optional)**

For filling, in a small saucepan stir together the sugar and flour. Add the milk; cook and stir till thickened and bubbly. Cook and stir for 1 minute more. Gradually stir *some* of the hot mixture into the egg. Return all to saucepan. Cook and stir till slightly thickened; reduce heat. Cook and stir 1 minute more but *do not boil*. Remove from heat.

Stir the ground almonds, butter or margarine, vanilla, and almond extract into the thickened mixture. Cool without stirring.

To assemble in a lapped fold, spoon ¼ of the filling in the center of the unbrowned side of a Basic Dessert Crêpe. Fold two opposite edges so they overlap atop filling (step 3). Repeat with remaining filling and crêpes.

Place the filled crêpes, seam side up, in a greased 7x5½x2-inch baking dish. Bake, uncovered, in a 350° oven for 10 to 15 minutes or till heated through. If desired, garnish crêpes with sliced toasted almonds. Makes 2 servings.

Saucy Apple Crêpes

If you are using tart apples, you may omit the lemon juice—

- 4 **Basic Dessert Crêpes (see recipe opposite)**
- 1 **medium cooking apple, cored and sliced**
- 1 **tablespoon butter *or* margarine**
- ½ **cup apple juice**
- 1 **tablespoon brown sugar**
- 1 **teaspoon lemon juice**
- ¼ **teaspoon ground cinnamon**

To fold the Basic Dessert Crêpes in a quarter fold, fold a crêpe in half, with the browned side to the outside. Fold in half again, forming a triangle; set aside. Repeat.

For sauce, in a small skillet cook the apple slices in hot butter or margarine about 5 minutes or till tender. Stir in the apple juice, brown sugar, lemon juice, and cinnamon. Cook and stir the mixture till the brown sugar is dissolved.

Arrange the crêpes atop sauce (step 4). Spoon the sauce over crêpes. Cook over low heat till heated through, spooning sauce over crêpes. Makes 2 servings.

Brandied Coffee

- 3 **inches stick cinnamon**
- 1 **tablespoon sugar**
- ¼ **teaspoon finely shredded orange peel**
- 3 **tablespoons brandy**
- 4 **teaspoons instant coffee crystals Pressurized dessert topping**

Combine 1½ cups *water,* cinnamon, sugar, and the orange peel. Cover and simmer for 5 minutes. Strain. Add the brandy and coffee crystals, stirring to dissolve coffee.

Top each serving with dessert topping. Makes 2 servings.

Equipment

When you're cooking for two, you should be thinking small. Equip your kitchen with small mixing bowls, skillets, saucepans, and baking dishes. Of course, you may need other sizes if you plan to entertain, but remember, it's more efficient to prepare and cook foods in containers that are scaled to the size of the recipe.

Mixing equipment: *Mixing bowls* are essential for beating and mixing small amounts of ingredients, especially eggs.

Cookware: When you cook on the range top, the size of container is crucial. Using a pan that is too big will cause excess evaporation and overcooking. The *6-inch* and *8-inch skillets* are excellent for sautéing vegetables, browning meats, and making omelets.

As for saucepans, you might want to have more than one of both the *1-quart* and *1½-quart saucepan* sizes.

Baking equipment: A must in any kitchen for two are *small casseroles* ranging in size from 10 ounces to 1½ quarts. Also for baking casseroles, desserts, and some quick breads, you may want several different sizes of baking dishes such as the *5x5x2-inch, 6½x6½x2-inch,* or *8x6½x2-inch baking dishes.*

When you want to bake a small cake or bread, there are a number of baking pans that will come to your rescue. For pound cakes, there are *4-inch individual fluted tube pans* in addition to all the baking dishes listed above. Bread can be baked in either a *6x3x2-inch loaf pan* or in *4½x2½x1½-inch individual loaf pans.* Loaf pans can also be used for pâtés, meat loaves, and layered foods.

When baking a cake or bread for two, cupcakes and muffins are often the best way to go. Both can be made in regular *muffin pans.*

Miscellaneous: Many different kinds of specialized cooking equipment are made for cooking in small quantities. Although designed for a specific purpose, they can often be used for several types of dishes.

You may want a *2-cup soufflé dish,* which can also hold a layered dessert or salad.

In addition to saucy foods, individual *au gratin dishes* make great containers for enchiladas, manicotti, and crêpes.

When you want to make individual servings of custards or puddings, you will find *6-ounce* and *10-ounce custard cups* to be invaluable. These versatile cups can also double as molds if you don't have individual *¾-cup molds.*

For savory and sweet pies or tarts you will probably want *4-inch* and *7-inch pie plates.* They can also serve as quiche dishes in case you don't have a *4-inch quiche pan.*

Appliances

Several appliances perform best when working with small amounts of food. Though they are not always necessary, they do speed up food preparation.

Mixer: A *hand-held electric mixer* is ideal for beating and mixing small amounts of ingredients. You'll find it especially valuable for beating an egg in a small mixer bowl.

Blender: A *blender* is another handy mixing appliance to have in the two-person kitchen. It actually functions at its best when blending small portions of food. Use the blender to make bread or cracker crumbs, chop nuts, puree fruit, grate cheese, and blend liquids.

Toaster oven: When you're cooking foods in small baking dishes, try using a *toaster oven.*

These compact units require minimal storage space and energy. Not only can you toast in your toaster oven, but you can also reheat, bake, and even broil in some models.

Microwave oven: If you're pushed for time, cook with a *counter-top microwave oven.* A silent third partner in your kitchen, the microwave oven will cook your two-portion servings about two or three times faster than the corresponding family-size recipes. Your microwave oven will also perform a variety of cooking tasks such as melting butter and toasting nuts.

Crockery cooker: The *electric slow crockery cooker* is another time-saver as it almost eliminates any last-minute food preparation. This stoneware pot simmers foods slowly, so the foods reach a flavorful peak by the time you're ready to eat. In addition to cooking roasts, casseroles, and stews, some models can also be used for fondue. The 3½-cup or 4-cup model will serve the two of you well.

Barbecue: For grilling, heat a *hibachi.* This small grill requires less charcoal than the larger grills and can be transported more easily on picnics.

Miscellaneous: A number of other appliances that cater to couples are available on the market. They range from *mini-deep-fat fryers* to *6-cup coffee makers.* Acquire them as they become necessary. Remember to consider storage space, and always buy the best quality you can afford.

Serving Sizes

FOOD	AMOUNT FOR TWO SERVINGS
BEEF and VEAL	
Beef short ribs	12 ounces
Bone-in beef or veal steaks (2 steaks)	½ pound
Boneless beef or veal and ground beef	½ pound
Dried or smoked beef	4 ounces
PORK, HAM and SAUSAGE	
Pork spareribs	12 ounces
Pork chops (2 chops)	12 ounces
Boneless pork and ground pork	½ pound
Boneless ham and Canadian-style bacon	½ pound (about 1 cup cubed)
Pork sausage	½ pound
Salami and Polish sausage	½ pound
LAMB	
Lamb chops (2 chops)	½ pound
Boneless lamb and ground lamb	½ pound
POULTRY	
Chicken breast	1 whole medium
Chicken thighs	4 medium
Chicken drumsticks	4 medium
Chicken legs	2 medium
Chicken livers	6 ounces
Diced cooked chicken or turkey	1 cup
Cornish hen	1 1- to 1½-pound hen
FISH and SEAFOOD	
Fish fillets	½ pound
Salmon, fresh	1 1-inch-thick steak
Canned salmon, tuna, or crab	about 7 ounces
Shucked clams or oysters	1 cup
Shelled shrimp	12 ounces
DAIRY PRODUCTS	
Eggs	4 large
Cheese (cheddar or Swiss)	4 ounces (1 cup shredded)
Soft cheeses (cream, cottage, ricotta)	4 ounces (1 cup)
RICE, PASTA, and CEREALS (Uncooked)	
Brown rice, wild rice, and long grain rice	⅓ cup
Quick-cooking rice	½ cup
Medium noodles	1 cup
Elbow macaroni	½ cup
Spaghetti	2 ounces
Pearl barley	¼ cup
Quick-cooking barley	⅓ cup
Quick-cooking rolled oats	¾ cup
Regular rolled oats	½ cup
Quick-cooking grits	½ cup
Bulgur wheat	⅓ cup
Packaged instant mashed potatoes	⅔ cup

Food Storage

Refrigerating or Freezing: Refrigerate or freeze your perishable foods as soon as possible. Once a food has been cooked, cover and refrigerate any leftovers promptly. To thaw frozen foods, place in the refrigerator or in a sealed bag under cold running water.

Meat, Poultry, Fish: Fresh meat and poultry wrapped in clear flexible packaging may be refrigerated as purchased. To freeze, remove this packaging; wrap in a moisture-vaporproof material. Wrap all fresh fish in moisture-vaporproof material to refrigerate or freeze.

Fruits, Vegetables: Generally, fresh fruits and vegetables are best stored in the refrigerator crisper. Keep staple vegetables such as potatoes, onions, and root vegetables in a cool, dry, well-ventilated place.

Freeze extra tomato paste, chopped onion, green pepper, and mushrooms in the amounts you would use when making a casserole or sauce. Freeze any leftover cooked vegetables for making soups and casseroles.

Dairy Products: When you are freezing cheese, remember, the harder the cheese, the longer the storage period. Because the texture of cheese changes and tends to be more crumbly after freezing, use the thawed cheese for cooking purposes. Do not freeze cottage cheese.

To refrigerate egg yolks, cover the unbeaten yolks with water before chilling. Be sure to beat both egg yolks and whole eggs before freezing. Egg whites can be refrigerated or frozen without beating. Store each egg white in a section of an ice cube tray for easy measurement.

Freeze dollops of whipped cream on a baking sheet. Put them in freezer containers to store in the freezer till needed. Remove dollops from containers and let them thaw about 20 minutes before serving.

FOOD	MAXIMUM STORAGE TIMES	
	Refrigerator (36°F. to 40°F.)	Freezer (0°F. or lower)
MEAT		
Beef	2 to 4 days	6 to 12 months
Pork	2 to 4 days	3 to 6 months
Ground meats	1 to 2 days	3 months
Ham	1 week	2 months
Bacon	5 to 7 days	1 month
Frankfurters	4 to 5 days	1 month
Fresh pork sausage	7 days	2 months
Smoked sausage	3 to 7 days	(do not freeze)
Dry sausage	2 to 3 weeks	(do not freeze)
Luncheon meats	1 week	(do not freeze)
Lamb	2 to 4 days	6 to 9 months
Veal	2 to 4 days	6 to 9 months
Variety meats	1 to 2 days	3 to 4 months
Cooked meats	4 to 5 days	2 to 3 months
POULTRY		
Chicken pieces	1 to 2 days	6 months
Cooked poultry	2 to 3 days	1 month
Cornish hen	1 to 2 days	6 to 12 months
FISH	1 to 2 days	4 months
BREADS		
Quick breads	2 to 4 days	2 months
Yeast breads	1 week	4 to 8 months
COOKIES and CAKES		
Cookies	3 to 5 days	12 months
Cookie dough	1 week	6 months
Cupcakes or cakes	1 week	4 to 8 months
DAIRY PRODUCTS		
Butter	2 weeks	3 to 6 months
Whole eggs	2 to 3 weeks	4 months (beaten only)
Egg yolks	2 days	4 months (beaten only)
Egg whites	10 days	6 months
Soft cheeses	5 days	1 month
Hard cheeses	1 month	2 months
Process cheeses	2 months	4 months
Whipping cream	2 to 3 days	(do not freeze)
Whipped cream	1 hour	3 months (in dollops)
PREPARED DISHES		
Casseroles	2 to 4 days	2 to 3 months
Soups and stews	2 to 4 days	6 months
SANDWICHES	1 to 2 days	2 weeks (Do not freeze sandwiches containing mayonnaise or tomatoes.)

Index

A-B

Index

Index